LEAD GREAT TEAMS

CHANGING CHALLENGES

INTO OPPORTUNITIES

WITH YOUR TEAM

BRANDON FULLER

Copyright © 2022

All rights reserved. No part of this publication may be reproduced, distributed, or transmitted in any form or by any means, including photocopying, recording, or other electronic or mechanical methods, without the prior written permission of the author of the book, except in the form of brief quotations embodied in critical reviews and certain other noncommercial purposes permitted by copyright law.

Author's Dedications

Foremost my savior Jesus Christ, for whom I gladly point the glory to. My amazing family, who have always been my greatest source of inspiration and motivation. Your unwavering love and support have helped me push myself to new heights. I am grateful for the guidance, encouragement, and unwavering belief in me.

Introduction

If you are looking for a "self-help" book, this book probably isn't for you. In some ways, the focus of this book is quite the opposite, it's geared toward helping provide context for enabling leadership by putting your own ambitions aside and focusing on *servant* leadership.

Although the vernacular of this book may be geared toward a business model, it has positive practical life applications as well.

Often, in the workplace, when you excel in your role or on your team, you may be identified for a management or leadership position. The thought here is if you've displayed excellence in one area, you should be able to excel when given more responsibility.

In most cases, no one outlines your next steps as a manager or leader before throwing you into the fire, ultimately expecting you to meet expectations as successfully as you did in your previous role. This changeover can be one of the hardest professional transitions you will make. The mindset shift is a completely differing set of cognitive skills, tools, and abilities, along with a somewhat ambiguous set of ideas for how to measure success. You may feel like an abandoned shipwrecked passenger left out at sea. It can feel intimidating or even defeating, meanwhile, you want to reach out for help to identify what area specifically needs adjustment. But who do you go to? This often leads to confusion about what to do to be successful in your new position and tends to ignite the fight-or-flight triggers in most. You can either buckle down and dig in, and through sheer willpower, make it work, or stay suspended in a spiraling role of ever-challenging chaos that never makes sense.

If this all sounds familiar, then this book is written for you. I want to outline some of the biggest identified areas for improvement and success that I learned as I leaned into the challenges. And I want to help you do the same.

To begin, don't believe everything you think. Moreover, leadership is a learned skill and not an inherent attribute. I often compare leadership to a paradox: leaders need to know every aspect of their area of industry while being open to the realization that they know almost nothing. Why is this important to understand? Because people are looking up to the leader to have the answers, and even when you (as the leader) don't have the answer, you need to know where to *find* the answer and keep momentum moving forward, while being open to change, but also knowing when to stand firm. Okay, I know that may seem like a lot to balance, and it is, but now that you know, I'm going to help you get better at it.

Leadership is an ever-changing target, which takes a lot of dedication, soft skills, and ability to make sound strategic decisions. As a leader, your team is of primary importance, so you need to know how to rely on them, trust them, and delegate work toward their skills and strengths.

The leader is the bridge builder to keep traffic moving. You must be humble while also flexible. You must be open to feedback and listen, while also knowing the best decisions to make. You must be respectful, while also gaining the respect of your team. You must be patient, while also having the ability to drive your team toward rapid success.

If you are ready for the challenge and the rewards that come from leadership, join me by diving into this book so you can strengthen your leadership skills. This book will help reinforce the leader that others see in you.

Some of the core reasons I am writing this book reside in the following statistics:

- With **more than 77%** of organizations reporting a gap in leadership, it's clear there's a critical need for effective leadership development.

- **83%** of businesses recognize the importance of building leadership skills at all levels, yet less than *5%* of companies are taking action to implement leadership development programs.
- This gap is particularly alarming when we consider that **47%** of the skills required for executive-level positions are predicted to be in short supply in the future.

Statistics based off: (Apollo Technical 2022)

In this book, we'll explore the root causes of the leadership gap, the impact it has on organizations, and practical strategies for developing the leadership skills needed to thrive in today's fast-paced business environment. There is a massive area of growth potential in the area of leadership, so it's time to take action and seize the opportunity to develop the skills and qualities that will make you an effective leader in today's rapidly changing world. This book will provide you with the insights, tools, and strategies you need to cultivate a strong leadership mindset, build high-performing teams, and achieve your organization's goals with confidence. Whether you're a seasoned executive or an emerging leader, the time to invest in your leadership development is now.

Lead Great Teams is all about finding the full potential of your team through effective leadership. By empowering your team members to achieve their best and work collaboratively toward shared goals, you can create a high-performing team culture that drives real results. As you dive into the pages ahead, you'll discover actionable insights and strategies for developing your leadership skills, building a cohesive team, and achieving success on a whole new level.

Leadership isn't just about being strong for the sake of strength. It's about empowering your team to be strong too. After all, at the heart of leadership lies your team. That's why this book is all about YOUR team - because they are the key to your *success*.

TABLE OF CONTENTS

TEAMWORK THAT INSPIRES DREAMWORK	14
LEADERSHIP	34
INFLUENCE OF LEADERSHIP ON ORGANIZATIONAL CULTURE	59
RECRUITING AND RETAINING	75
GAME THEORY	105
STRATEGIZING WITH PSYCHOLOGY	124
SOFT SKILLS IN THE TEAM	136
COMPONENTS OF EFFECTIVE SOCIAL INTELLIGENCE IN LEADERSHIP	160
LEAN STARTUP & AGILE MANAGEMENT	179
ARE LEADERS BORN OR MADE?	192
THE SCIENCE BEHIND A SUCCESSFUL, EFFICIENT, AND PRODUCTIVE TEAM	206
THE MEASURE OF SUCCESS	224
CLOSING STATEMENTS	238
REFERENCES	239

Chapter 1

Teamwork That Inspires Dreamwork

"It is the fuel that allows common people to attain uncommon results."

-Andrew Carnegie

Everyone has the capacity and potential to achieve something great in life - they just need to recognize what drives their passion and interest and utilize it in a way that helps them cross the finish line and meet their goals. The sculptor Michelangelo once said, "In every block of marble, I see a statue as plain as though it stood before me, shaped and perfect in attitude and action. I have only to hew away the rough walls that imprison the lovely apparition to reveal it to the other eyes as mine see it."

Much in the same way, that certainty of outcome is what a great leader is able to see in others and can harness for a beneficial outcome. We can read books about leadership, get a degree, and attend seminars, but in the end, we will still lack something that keeps us from being effective leaders if we can't connect and utilize that deep passion that innately resides in truly great leaders. Great leaders see the true value in others and through efficient, effective, and skillful planning and coordination, can produce quality results and add value to whatever they are working on. Through teamwork, leaders orchestrate goals that would otherwise be unaccomplishable, as there is no better way than teamwork.

Inevitably, you will encounter challenges in your career where you may not achieve your goals with your team, leading to feelings of regret. Such situations can arise for various reasons and may even cause disagreements within your team. However, it's essential to view these challenges as opportunities for growth in your leadership journey. Instead of dwelling on failures, use them as stepping-stones to advance your leadership skills and turn challenges into valuable learning experiences.

Employee and Team Engagement (Wins the Day)

A team is made up of individuals who each serve a unique purpose (or potentially several purposes) to reach an identified goal. It can be challenging to build a healthy team environment due to each member's different personality, level of skill, and differing prior experiences, but it is exactly these differences that are highly beneficial once you have worked through the initial team-building phases using healthy communication skills and patience, which in turn become instilled in the team.

In order to equip each team member with the appropriate tools to execute with excellence on your team, it is your responsibility as a leader to equip them with proper training to bring the desired pace in alignment with expectations. Each team member's understanding of the process should be strong enough to proceed in their role.

As a team leader, it is necessary to offer some sort of incentive to the team members as it pushes them to enhance their performance and be more productive. Even little positive remarks of encouragement can go a long way, but the complete absence of incentive can kill motivation.

After a hard day's work, team members may feel under-appreciated, leading to lower morale and decreased loyalty to the team's goals. This is the most common cause for breakdowns in teamwork that inevitably lead to failure, which also proves as an important area to focus encouragement toward.

If you don't offer an appropriate level of encouragement, you may want to rethink your process. A team is not supposed to work without the determination to achieve, simply for a mere salary, with zero interest in the goal. When you create an unbreakable connection with your team via private and public acknowledgment and strong communication, it becomes your extended family.

A Team is a Force Multiplier

A team is an essential key to your success, which can lead you to extraordinary results. You don't make a team; you build it. Investing your days and nights working solo on any project means you focus on one requirement at a time. Sooner or later, it will inevitably start draining your energy, become overly taxing, and prevent the ability to scale for efficiency and performance. It is also very difficult to keep yourself motivated while working alone – and you are also limited to your own ideas.

Now, let's explore an analogy that sheds light on the importance of simplicity towards understanding foundational elements in business. Imagine a blank puzzle representing a business, with each person in the organization symbolizing a unique puzzle piece necessary for completion. In this analogy, the value of the business lies in the collective completion of the puzzle, where no single person is more or less important than the others. Only when the business operates at a stable and successful level does the puzzle reveal its complete picture.

Importance of each role...

Each person has a unique and pivotal purpose for the completion of the business puzzle. No one person in the business is any more or less important than the other. No single person can complete the puzzle with their single piece, but the interworking of all the pieces is where the value of the business exists.

The nature of the puzzle being blank exists in the analogy because as a business matures and understands its full purpose (in the market) to completion, the puzzle can then be articulated to a complete picture (the business is operating at a stable, successful level). Only once the full operation (completion of the puzzle) is complete can you start replicating and extending the purpose of the puzzle. The need to understand and fully "operate" the business is a necessity before building additional complexity (taking on additional pieces).

This is where the concept of simplicity before additional complexity comes into play. A business that keeps reaching for more before it has fully understood its foundational pieces is destined to fall apart. This is just like a mismatched puzzle - attempting to take pieces from additional puzzles that were carved out too early to understand the completion of the parts working together as a whole.

When you have a team, every team member lifts each other up during the process, but you don't have this luxury while working individually. Working alone can be challenging, especially when it comes to managing your time effectively. The burden of work falls solely on your shoulders, making it harder to stay productive and creative. But there's a bigger problem at play here—working in isolation can take a toll on your mental health, leaving you stressed and uninspired. That's why engagement during work is crucial - not only does it lead to new ideas and fresh perspectives, it can also alleviate stress if done correctly.

Teamwork allows you to divide duties among those with expertise in that area, which makes the work more efficient and provides more time for you and each team member to focus on the tasks they are best suited to. Efficiency, effectiveness, and productivity is the long-term payoff.

Use your time on what is most important.

When you're building your skill set, you need to be practicing what you're learning as often as you possibly can. Without taking the opportunity to put yourself in a career position where you can practice this early and often, you're losing a tremendous opportunity. Each day lost has a compounding effect. Much in the same way, the skills you learn can be built onto each other perpetually into the future, gaining you more invaluable knowledge for further opportunities.

Time is a super precious resource, more so even than any monetary resource.

When the tasks are distributed among the team members (*who have the knowledge and skills to accomplish their duties accurately*), it creates the possibility of generating more progress, results, and potentially more revenue. The money spent on four different people working together for the same goal can produce the result of ten people working individually as everyone will have their own set of skills, focusing only on that. (VisioneerIT n.d.)

This tends to produce the "Multiplier Effect," which can only be achieved through effective teamwork. Team members working in consonance with multiplier capabilities can easily increase profitability.

Let's suppose there is a group of five prospective marketing students who were assigned to sell 60 products in three days. Managers divide the sets of products equally in the group. They also sort out the duties of every member **according to their skill set**. One must *market* the product, the other would be required to *communicate* with the customer, the third one *negotiates/sells*, the fourth performs accounting for the products, and the fifth one is positioned to be in charge of strategy due to their expertise in that area. The group members now have three days to sell the products. The pressure gets equally distributed, so it becomes easier to increase sales and complete the assignment faster and in a more engaging (*fun*), efficient, and effective manner.

Together, there is potential for a much ***better*** outcome. This is a simple and contrite example, and the positive factors may not be immediately obvious, but as the effect is scaled, so is the value from the principle. A team, a good team, is so much more valuable in scale than anything you can do by yourself. Create a team that can help you grow and who understands your plan—a team that cares about the vision as much as you do.

Diverse Perspectives Solve Problems More Efficiently

Every person in the world comes with unique creative originality and capabilities which can be used in multiple areas (*and to multiply efficiency and effectiveness* – like compound interest for projects). No one person can be an expert in everything, and there will always be others who are better, faster, or more creative in certain areas. Collaborating with others can help you tap into their unique strengths and abilities, opening up new opportunities and perspectives you may not have considered before.

Teamwork brings diversity and accountability to your work.

Because you have multiple opinions and ideas in a team, the work can be executed more efficiently and effectively, and the learning opportunities increase as each person brings unique ideas to the table. The unique backgrounds offered by differing individuals on the team can serve as an ever-growing center of creativity, innovation, and ingenuity.

Building a team consisting of people with unique skill sets and educational backgrounds can introduce creative ways to solve a problem. Each person can offer a uniquely different perspective when looking at challenges and can offer solutions according to their understanding.

When you create a team where every person feels comfortable giving their input according to their skill set (and passion), you come across ideas you would never have considered otherwise. Different and diverse perspectives can turn what once seemed unattainable into a surprising but welcome reality.

When gathered collectively to work on the same project, people from different areas with different knowledge have a higher chance of reaching the top in less time than those who work by themselves.

Benefits of Servant Leadership

Have you ever had the chance to experience growth and support in your field? If so, it's hard to *unsee* the tremendous results. Teamwork allows you to expand your abilities and promote yourself further to uncover previously hidden opportunities. But how is that possible? A good leader will focus on what a team member can contribute to the goal rather than putting extra burden on them. They will be more interested in team member engagement (which will lead to productivity) and provide guidance every step of the way. But it is not as easy as it sounds. The leader should be capable enough to instill a level of comfort among the team members that prevents them from feeling isolated. Team members should feel psychologically safe enough to share their thoughts or ask for help if they feel stuck.

With teamwork, healthy communication is vital. Be calm and humble, listen to each person, and acknowledge their thoughts. Walk with them on the path to create a better understanding between everyone.

When we look at companies that have demonstrated success (in the traditional sense of *corporate success*), there is one common theme - the efforts they make to create a positive workplace environment. These companies truly believe in their people's satisfaction and support a work culture that increases productivity and quality of work. A major reason they have become successful is that they created a family environment between employees, which leads to extraordinary results. (Akorede 2018) According to research, 86% of Google employees are satisfied with their jobs. More than 64,000 employees in Google are provided additional company benefits. According to PayScale, 73% of Google employees find their jobs worth their time. (Gillett 2016) But these concepts don't have to be limited to Google or other big-name companies. We can integrate those concepts and skill sets into our own work for the benefit of our teams.

Your team will perform better if they are valued and know their efforts are not wasted. If a team member's work is acknowledged, it will boost their energy, and they will contribute more readily to accomplish the goals set forth. Every person wants to contribute to something meaningful and purposeful.

As a leader, if your team members make a mistake, allow them to learn from it and move forward. This is an opportunity to build trust.

It is also important to identify where your team is lacking and then provide them with the right feedback and guidance to bring them back on track so that they continue to contribute to the team. It is essential to give them time to understand and let them become comfortable in the team, but it is also important to recover expediently when a problem occurs.

However, it is wise to identify those who are not a good fit for the team as early as possible and replace them. As it is brilliantly explained by Jim Collins in his book *Good to Great*, "Letting the wrong people hang around is unfair to all the right people, as they inevitably find themselves compensating for the inadequacies of the wrong people. Worse, it can drive away the best people. Strong performers are intrinsically motivated by performance, and when they see their efforts impeded by carrying extra weight, they eventually become frustrated." (Collins, Good to Great n.d.)

We should build a team similar to how we raise a child—in an environment of encouragement and teaching with patience. We are nurturing an intelligent mind, providing sustenance, and showing patience during the team-building process. This encourages a team of diverse mindsets who work together to accomplish their goals. We need patience to deal with every difficulty and ensure the team stays strong. It is the leader's duty not to let anyone give up.

There are some things in life you can do without outside support or people helping you, but not everything can be done alone. Aligning with the team to distribute the responsibilities isn't considered *weakness*. Instead, frame your mind around the potential of **scalability**. It is more like building a union for a common goal than taking it as being weak in certain areas. It changes from *your* mission to the *team's* mission.

On the other side of this, you can't expect to recruit help from just *anyone*... You need the right people aligned with the right jobs. Building a team is not simply gathering a random set of people to help, it is a big responsibility and a long endeavor.

If we provide the same set of tasks to ten different people, each may have a unique approach to performing it. The result might be similar, but the way of achieving the goal may be astonishingly different. Some objectives will take longer, but with the long-term goal in mind, the work is well worth the effort. When it comes to achieving a common goal, there's normally not one "right" way—a good team will draw on a variety of strategies and skill sets to cross the finish line in their own unique way. From brainstorming sessions to last-minute implementations, every step of the journey is a chance for the team to showcase their strengths and bring their vision to life. This helps to prove there are several ways of doing a job.

Results can become more efficient by working smarter rather than harder because the scalability factors have a maximizing benefit factor that can outweigh the most diligent hard work. Thus, you must recognize abilities and distribute the work accordingly. The leader must prioritize the use of every member effectively, or it will *not* benefit the team in any way.

In our daily lives, most of us solve our fundamental problems by discussing them with a close friend or family member. We seek a different perspective from someone who can *objectively* review our issues with an *external* mindset. And when the situation you were facing is solved, that is referred to as teamwork. Whether we work with an informal or formal team, there's always more than one person involved in the process.

Going Further *Together*...Not Alone

Sometimes we think we know everything there is to know about our work and that no one can do it better than us. With this approach, we are not only slowing down the process but also limiting our ability to learn something new.

There's always room for growth, no matter how far we have reached. Never stop learning; always push further. Working with several people strengthens our journey to success and enables us to learn more. Involving great minds from every corner of the world and bringing them together attracts opportunity, diversity, and creativity.

Working alone toward a goal has many disadvantages, including additional stress related to the burden of tasks, opportunity cost loss, limited ability to think creatively and objectively, and a limited ability to produce innovative results. Most people tend to stick to the same routine, which obstructs progress. As convenient as it sounds, over time it becomes the opposite and affects the outcome.

As a leader, you know firsthand that success doesn't come without its fair share of personal challenges. There are days when you might feel like throwing in the towel and pursuing a different path. But it's in those moments of struggle that your leadership truly shines. By persevering and staying consistent and committed to your goals, you inspire your team to do the same and emerge stronger on the other side.

Putting it All Together

Teamwork is centered in humility while promoting progress, sustainability, and relationships. A team tends to operate better under minimal constraints and when it offers a safe place to speak and be heard. Most brilliant ideas result from brainstorming and open discussions in a cohesive environment. When negativity sneaks in, a team's bonding starts to weaken. So, it is better to practice empathy and self-control (especially as a leader) and focus on the bigger picture.

> *Scalable and successful projects require and are based on teamwork, our ability to adapt, learning from years of attempts, gathered knowledge, and successive findings. It is a collective effort of people willing to work for a common goal to bring change.*

Great things don't happen instantaneously - it takes courage, diligence, and a lot of work to build something from nothing, and this kind of strength comes from the support of people who believe in one common goal and ambition.

Additional Thoughts

A team is defined as multiple people working together to accomplish a common objective by collaborating on related projects. In order to establish a harmonious workplace and foster teamwork, it is necessary to forge valuable relationships with the team members. Correspondence and agreeable connections will shape a productive working environment where partnerships are useful, meaningful, inspiring, and promoting opportunity to willingly collaborate with one another. Employees can improve their work performance and reduce issues that dampen the team's work momentum in such an atmosphere. A team member's sense of belonging increases when there is synchronicity in the workplace.

Maintaining healthy relationships with coworkers can sometimes fall by the wayside as pressure to complete tasks and meet deadlines increases. Teams can put the needs of their strategic work ahead of their own self-care. Neglecting relationships can significantly impact the performance of the team as a whole.

CHAPTER 2

Leadership

Your value on the team, in many cases, is not assessed by how well you can do your job, but rather how well you help the team efforts lead to success - in whatever capacity that is.

Leadership is the process of developing a vision, engaging with other team members' interests that lead toward the goal(s), and building each team member's motivation to achieve the leader's vision. To maintain the growth of the business, a leader must possess the right skills to guide others.

Individuals who combine leadership skills and interpersonal abilities have a unique advantage in leading a team. By doing so, they can discover new opportunities and add significant value to the team, making them an essential asset. Improving one's skills to become a better leader and making leadership a strong competency can make a person an even more valuable workplace member. Leadership capabilities, and soft skills relating to leadership, are among the most versatile toolsets you can obtain. Being a leader fundamentally sets you apart from others and allows you exponential potential for future opportunity.

I would much rather take an opportunity that promised growth in leadership skills (and fine-tuning them) over any monetary potential that doesn't help me grow. The reason is directly linked with the long-term goals assessment and the future opportunities it produces. The *invaluable* experience you get from growing as a leader, sharpening your skills as a leader, and/or learning from someone who improves your leadership skills will amount to astronomically more in the future than any job limiting your growth potential. The monetary trade-off may seem to be better in the short term, but the dividends the leadership experience offers you in the long run are well worth the trade.

There is a difference between being a leader and being a *good* leader. The latter focuses potential for leading a group of people to a specific goal or target. It is not *difficult* to be a leader of people, but to become a good leader requires an investment of time and requires some skill refinement. I want to take you on a journey to help you reflect on what it takes to be, not only a leader with passion and purpose that people follow because they *want* to and not because they *have* to.

Efficacious leaders understand the value of keeping discipline in the work environment by uniting the greater effort for the goals of the team, attempting to minimize any excess overage (risk mitigation), and attempting to meet or exceed timelines set out for deadlines as often as possible to reach the desired result. Keeping an objective view of time in mind, a good leader can save their employees from task and work overload by distributing work appropriately due to well-planned and organized efforts. When the team leader values time and can keep everyone on track, the team will have more potential to produce a quality result.

A functional leader will ensure that the team members are aware of their tasks and the time provided. It needs to be appropriately structured for everyone. To maintain this, you need thoughtful planning, productive communication with the team, and the ability to intercede if something does not go according to the plan (which happens quite often). These qualities will save from rushing the outcome and performing better while being on time. Relying on a last-ditch effort to achieve results in the final moments may work occasionally, but it is not a sustainable long-term strategy. If you find yourself frequently in these high-pressure situations, it may be time to reassess your approach and make changes. That often is where mistakes happen. Making last-minute decisions is tough, and having to make multiple last-minute decisions on frequent occasions (due to a lack of adequate planning) is a recipe for disaster. But when it happens, take ownership, lead with composure, and do the best with the opportunity you have. Leadership is all about making the best out of what you have been given.

Good leaders denote courage, especially in difficult times. The ability to adapt to the changes and instantly think of ways of recovery, rather than panicking about every setback should be avoided by a leader. It can help the team to find a silver lining in the situation and won't sacrifice the harmony of the project.

The astute leader sees challenges as opportunities. A calm leader, confident in their abilities, takes a step back and begins to see opportunities in difficult circumstances rather than panic. These leaders can quickly identify the root causes of difficulties and provide expedient solutions. They are then able to open up and expand into previously undiscovered opportunities that could have prevented the difficulty in the first place. When a leader does not maintain composure, crisis frequently ensues, leading to clouded judgment and rushed decisions.

Avoid falling into immaturity or lack of preparedness when leading, particularly during times of uncertainty, adversity, crisis, and change. This will make others around you feel unsafe and insecure. Here are seven ways to keep your cool as a leader even when things get tough:

1. Don't Let Emotions Rule (*Use Emotional Intelligence*)

Leaders with experience know not to have their emotions on display (*or at least without intentionality*). When things get tough, they don't yell or get too anxious. These leaders maintain emotional self-control, reflected in their body language. They remain composed and seldom allow their emotions to show without a specific purpose. I often like to compare business and leadership to a high-stakes poker game. In many ways, you can't show all your cards, but it does require a great deal of confidence to model behavior and drive your vision toward success.

Employees interpret this as evidence that you are not being sufficiently objective and overly passionate about the situation when you allow your feelings to get in the way. Effective leaders strike a balance between expressing concern and maintaining composure. While they possess a strong will, they never allow their emotions to become a distraction or interfere with their ability to handle situations responsibly and objectively.

2. Don't Take Things Personally

It can be difficult to maintain composure and convince those around you that you have everything under control when you start to take things personally. Leadership requires the ability to remain objective while making decisions based on what's best for the organization or team rather than allowing oneself to be influenced by personal feelings or biases. When leaders become too emotionally invested in a situation, they may lose their ability to think rationally and make sound decisions.

Acknowledging this tendency and actively working to avoid taking things too personally can help leaders stay focused on what's most important. It allows them to maintain their composure in difficult situations, which can be reassuring to those around them. It also enables them to remain objective and avoid making decisions based on personal biases or emotions.

3. Keep a Positive Mental Attitude

A leader's actions, behavior, and overall demeanor are constantly being observed by their employees and peers. Leaders must maintain a positive outlook and manage consistency that inspires and fuels their employees during the most difficult times. By remaining steadfast, positive, and authentically displaying a sense of compassion, your leadership experience and resolve can shine in almost any situation.

The tone of an organization is set by its leaders. A leader's ability to make course corrections in the face of adversity can be the change that makes all the difference but requires adopting a positive position. During times of uncertainty, employees benefit from these leaders' positive attitudes. Maintain a positive mental attitude and watch the team grow.

4. REMAIN FEARLESS

As a leader, demonstrating a sense of calmness and composure in the face of adversity can have a profound impact on the overall team, enabling them to remain focused and productive even during difficult times.

Remaining fearless as a leader is not about ignoring the risks or challenges that lie ahead. Rather, it is about acknowledging those risks and challenges and taking decisive action to address them. It is about being willing to take calculated risks and make tough decisions, even in the face of uncertainty.

One of the key components of remaining fearless as a leader is the ability to stay focused on the big picture. It's easy to get bogged down in the day-to-day details and lose sight of the larger goals and objectives. By maintaining a clear perspective on what truly matters, leaders can make decisions aligned with the organization's overall strategy and goals.

5. Respond Decisively

Leaders who keep their cool will limit the level of doubt they allow to creep in. They speak with authority, confidence, and conviction, regardless of whether they know the answer. They assure the team that everything is under control just by the way they deliver the message.

6. Take Accountability

When they are fully involved in resolving the issue at hand, leaders are at their calmest during times of crisis and change. When you say that you are accountable, it means that you have decided to take responsibility for the situation and do what needs to be done to solve it before it gets out of hand.

7. Posture Yourself Into The Scenario, Like You Have Been There Before

Great leaders are aware that preemptively setting yourself into a hypothetical scenario (before you end up in it) can help keep you calm during trying times. Those with strong executive presence who take the issue at hand with a sense of elegance and grace are leaders who demonstrate that they have been through the process of problem-solving numerous times before. They have patience, are active listeners, and will genuinely show compassion to alleviate the difficulties that others are going through.

Pay attention to the mentors and advisors that you learn from, and take a moment to really focus on how they carry themselves and how adept they are at relieving stress. You will probably find that in most cases they act in a way that suggests they have previously been there and that you feel at ease with their calm demeanor.

If you allow concern to turn into worry, and in turn, allow worry to culminate into fear, it is quite easy to lose your composure during times of crisis and change. The best leaders are capable of stepping back, critically evaluating the cards they have been dealt, and facing problems head-on because they keep their composure. A calm demeanor not only makes those you lead feel at ease but also fosters a safe and secure work environment where no one needs to panic in the face of adversity.

Calm leaders can influence the team more and encourage better results. For an employee, it is important to be aware of the position they stand in. As a leader, maintaining a calm and collected presence can foster trust and loyalty among team members, leading to increased productivity and success. They will have the surety of relying on their leaders in challenging times because they know how their leader will react and handle the situation in an objective and well-led manner. This behavior can be approached through multiple methods, and one of them is to consider the long-term repercussions and outcome of your position in the situation.

The Finer Points of Leadership

Each interaction you have as a leader reflects in a manner that either helps to drive or stall the progress to the goal. So, you must fully think through your actions and consider your available options as well-strategized responses. A well-thought and calculated response is consistently better than sudden reactions. And when you are confident about your approach, it will be well-received by the team members as well. Look into the problem thoroughly and decide accordingly based on the situation.

There is no shame in admitting when you don't have the answers to the problems the team is facing. It is not humanly possible to keep up with the fast changes in the world of business (and guessing sets the wrong precedent). But as a leader, when you share your concerns with the team and ask for their help, it will create unity among the team and leader, and foster collaboration and ownership. Containing your emotions when they are tested is a sign of a powerful leader with a strong influence on the team. Being resilient can build a good connection with the team, as a leader will inspire more understanding and create a friendly bond between the members. A leader's reaction to a complicated scenario mirrors an employee's behavior. The more this mindset is observed from the leader, the more the team will be receptive to displaying that same response themselves. Resilience will also lead you to growth for a healthy workplace.

While working in a team, it is expected that the team members or the leader will make mistakes (*and will even encourage mistakes to facilitate growth*). A leader who knows the values of a team's efforts tends to react humbly in these situations. Appreciate your employees' progress and ignore their mistakes *sometimes*. It will maintain the stability of the team morale and increase the leader's respect in the team's eyes (within moderation). This may sound counter-intuitive, and mind you, this is a long-term strategy, but I assure you that embracing mistakes can produce better results from employees over time. It emboldens employee ownership, helps nurture a feeling of safety, and encourages growth. Employees will be more vocal about their endeavors in the future rather than hiding them in fear. When you encounter setbacks, take it as a chance to improve and educate—while also encouraging growth. It is better to know the shortcomings of your team so you can strengthen and overcome them on time before incurring any long-term damage. It will also allow understanding of where your team and leader stand and what areas require improvement.

One of the most important soft skills a valuable leader can learn is the ability to work collaboratively. While working on a project with a team, the opinion of each member of the team matters. A leader should always be considerate of each team member's ideas and listen with an open mind. When a leader creates an open space for everyone to share their thoughts and opinions about a particular situation, it enables more creativity. And the employees will feel involved deeper in the team and the organization. Not only that, but it also decreases the stress of looking for answers from a single person. When a comfortable and safe environment is built, it creates more learning opportunities for everyone. It is unfair and unwise to expect all the answers from one person; people can only think according to their knowledge and expertise and are in many ways limited to their own prior experience. When an individual is burdened to think for everyone and solve problems, this puts a lot of pressure on that person, which in turn, can lead to wrong decisions and a lack of creativity.

Brainstorming with the team members can present more sound solutions than individualized thinking, which will allow members to think freely without the fear of being judged or intimidated and motivates them to participate in decision-making. This can bring more ideas to the table quickly. When the author Alex Osborn introduced the concept of brainstorming in his book *Applied Imagination: Principles and Procedures of Creative Thinking*, he came up with a technique called "Applied Imagination." He introduced some rules in this book, which include:

- Ideas can't be criticized.
- A goal is to collect many ideas.
- Appreciate experimental ideas.
- Move forward based on the ideas shared.

Osborn concluded that when these rules were practically followed, it increased the number of perspectives and improved the quality. This makes brainstorming more effective than just depending on one person. With this approach, you may find a new way of doing things you wouldn't have thought of otherwise. Sometimes receiving multiple perspectives can develop an alternative plan other than relying on a single plan.

Most entrepreneurs, innovators, and leaders hire managers to look after their work responsibilities *after* establishing a business. However, the concepts relating to management and leadership have inadvertently converged to be synonymous, although the two are not the same. There are many significant differences between a manager and a leader.

Management must, to a certain extent, direct or control employees and workers to meet a specific goal. Leadership, on the other hand, is about one's ability to create and foster an atmosphere of motivation and influence and encourage employees to provide their best for the company's betterment. These qualities of *influencing* and *inspiring* employees differentiate leadership from management. A leader does not try to hoard control or power. A leader has the capability (and, in many ways, the foresight) to create momentum and direction for the team and inspires them so that they work wholeheartedly. It can be challenging to be a leader and juggle being an efficient manager simultaneously or vice versa. Being a manager means taking control of the team and commanding them to work, which usually is not an inspiring technique - the leader's job is the opposite of that. Being a leader is all about flexibility and providing room to improve and work together in a safe, constructive environment. When a leader tries to adopt a manager's responsibilities or the other way around, it rarely results in success and will often confuse employees about the goals and their guidance.

Leaders are inventive. They create innovative ways to achieve growth for an organization. A leader focuses on where the company stands (and where it can be positioned in the future), what additional measures they must take, and how they can utilize their team to objectively reach those goals. But if we compare this to the manager, their sole focus is on creating a structure, looking into budgeting, and maintaining staff by a specific process. Managers tend to be restricted to *applying* strategies, making tasks/work, and developing plans to reach the goal made *by a leader*. The leader creates and defines the path, while the manager follows it. Regardless of the differences, they both have a significant role in an organization. Much in the same way, every person in the organization is essential for the organization as a whole.

To achieve their goals, managers align projects and rational processes. They take the available resources and make use of them. The manager divides time-intensive work into small tasks to complete them within a defined time. Contrastingly, a leader is interested in *influencing* the individuals on the team and how to align them with the goal, instead of just assigning them duties or tasks. They move forward in this journey by being side-by-side with the employees, teaching the team to work to the best of their abilities in important areas while learning to expect a better outcome from their hard work. The leader is also constantly looking for opportunities for team improvement. It's the difference between long-term and short-term strategy.

The manager is appointed to a specific position in a company, but a leader has a broader opportunity base. Your performance can lead you to leadership. If a person is capable enough to inspire others to give their best, then they have the opportunity to be considered a leader in a multitude of capacities. Regardless of the designation, you are hired. However, a manager has a fixed responsibility under a particular position.

For perspective, everyone is a *leader of something*. We may not be directly positioned in our daily employment as a leader, but we have the potential to lead. Make choices that reflect good decisions based on your leadership skills. Decisions are made constantly, and those decisions affect others – this is an act of leadership (intentionally or not).

Lead with purpose, intention, and passion.

Show others you can be trusted with the ability to lead (a decision, a team, a company, an organization, your family, your friends).

Leadership has the power to impact people's actions. It can motivate a group of people to see a future goal they can achieve. Leaders build visions in people's minds and influence them to reach the desired goal of an organization. A leader creates a climate in the workplace. They continuously focus on fixing the environment or the climate so the team is comfortable while at work and able to think creatively. According to author Keith Davis, "Leadership is the ability to persuade others to seek defined objectives enthusiastically. It is the human factor that binds a group together and motivates it towards goals."

77% of organizations recognize a gap in their current leadership,

83% feel leadership is important,

while **less than 5%** of companies focused on implementing leadership development.

Statistics based off: (Apollo Technical 2022)

Leaders are capable of making an impact with long-lasting effects. Take time to strategically think about how some of your choices have impacted you (positively and negatively). Think through how some of those decisions could have been curtailed or aligned to guide a different outcome for the affected result. Then take a few steps back and realize how you can use that capability to positively impact those around you and your team—and how utilizing that team's capabilities together can make an even more meaningful impact. This book is written with that in mind—harnessing the capabilities of a team—utilizing a collective set of skills to accomplish even greater things.

When looking at the development stages of a leader, one of the most pivotal and obvious levels that always stands out is their continuous aptitude and willingness to push the boundaries of learning. Leaders focus on their learning every step of the way. They try to learn something new every day. Their passion for improvement drives them. And invariably, they prefer to learn from the best in the industry. Their minds are so involved in improvement that they never miss a chance to catch something important, whether it be hearing out an innovative idea, mentors, other leaders, or books. Businesses in the U.S. invest $166 billion each year on the development of leadership, almost half of the $366 billion in global expenditures. ((Zippia) 2023)

The leader must be able to inspire the team to reach places far from their comforts (but within their abilities). Effectively leading the team creates hope of achieving unimaginable success for an organization. Leadership is a *stream of possibilities*, knowing which path to lead with is at the *delta* of each branch.

As a leader, it's not unreasonable to expect the ability to impact and influence others throughout the organization. But the leader must have reasonable expectations on their level of influence when starting in their role. Know your current role and ability for your level of influence. For instance, a mid-level manager is going to have a direct impact and influence on their team and potentially the teams around them. While a CEO may have an impact and influence on an *entire company*—but at a much different strategic objective and overall level. The focus levels are quite different, and so are the methods in which to implement them. It is not just about the level of reach or the position level that commands influence – it is also the *need* of the position. They are vastly different, yet both are still leaders. Both roles are necessary, and although they may seem disproportional, they are directionally aimed toward the same effect and outcome. Each role targets different areas of influence, but that is not to say you won't influence outside that capacity – it is simply more challenging to accomplish. But that is what drives leaders—the challenge to grow, succeed, and push the limits.

Additional Thoughts

The art of inspiring a group of people to work toward a common objective is the focus of leadership. This involves directing coworkers and employees with a plan to satisfy the requirements of the business. The foundations of leadership are captured in the capability and preparedness to inspire others.

A leader motivates and directs the actions of others. They need to be approachable enough for others to follow their orders, and they also need to be able to think critically to figure out the best way to make use of an organization's resources.

The art of persuading and influencing others to accept the group's goals is leadership. To be an effective leader, certain fundamental qualities are essential, such as the ability to connect with peers, direct subordinates, mediate disputes, make sound decisions by evaluating different options, allocate resources efficiently, and take calculated risks. Without these traits, it is difficult for leaders to maximize their potential and lead their teams to success.

Leadership can be viewed as the process of influencing others to achieve a goal and steering the organization in a way that strengthens its cohesiveness. By effectively utilizing leadership skills—beliefs, values, ethics, character, and knowledge/experience, leaders complete this process.

Chapter 3

Influence Of Leadership on Organizational Culture

Culture, in part, is defined by the achievements, norms, values, customs, and general beliefs of a particular group of people. In contrast, when we talk about organizational culture, it involves a company's work environment. This type of culture is about the mindsets and behaviors of the employees that contribute to the day-to-day functioning of the company.

Organizational culture incorporates objectives and mission with the values, expectations of employees, and leadership, as well as structured performance management and engagement levels. Companies with strong organizational cultures often have a better understanding of the direction and consistency of the work, better guidance of future decisions, and build positive and healthy energy in the work environment.

Organizational culture spans to every facet of the company, from employee benefits to punctuality and performance. When the culture is built according to the employee's advantages, it compliments their work, provides comfort and support, and makes them feel valued. Companies that consider culture essential are more likely to handle critical situations more wisely, have engaged employees, have healthier employees, and retain their employees.

Organizational culture can make or break a business, and it's something every member of the organization must be cognizant of. Whether you're a newcomer or a seasoned veteran, the culture's impact on you only grows stronger over time. In this way, the culture becomes not just a part of the organization, but a part of you.

But to maintain an effective organizational culture, you must keep in tune with your employees or direct reports about their ideas and concerns and communicate to them properly through active listening. Being intentional about organizational culture helps quantify (measure) and qualify (improve) the employee experience. Though it is hard work, the company's culture *can* be improved with time, and constant communication efforts with your team can have a ripple effect throughout the entire organization. When it's a time of critical importance, guide them by giving constructive critique and being present while going through different situations. It is not impossible to change organizational culture; all it takes is the determination to improve. Building a strong organizational culture is not an easy job, it needs serious work from leadership (regardless of job title), and it needs to be front of mind for every significant move a team takes.

Having said that, investing your time in an organization's growth will enable you to achieve greater results and keep the business in the right direction. In many ways, the organization's trajectory can be tuned accordingly and appropriately for a strategic outcome, but you need to know your goals. Understanding your goals and your ability, in line with your team's capability, is of primary importance.

Digging deeper: The Effects of Leadership.

Have you ever been to a store or a restaurant and noticed that even though they may be doing similar things as a competitor, the experience between the two is wildly different (chaotic, slow, poor service, etc.)? My mind is fixated on this type of thing and tends to focus on areas of improvement in processes, sociology, and psychology.

I frequently visited two separate restaurants that offered similar menus, yet the experiences at these establishments were vastly different. The first restaurant seemed to lack employee engagement and a sense of urgency. Orders took longer to fulfill, portion sizes varied inconsistently, and the overall experience was often marred by changing elements like the music or seating arrangements. In contrast, visiting the second restaurant for a nearly identical meal provided a completely different experience. The staff effortlessly delivered exceptional service with efficiency, consistency, and simplicity. It felt as though they always knew what they were doing and had a clear plan for success.

This stark contrast left me pondering: What made the difference? The two restaurants were located in the same geographic area, had access to a similar pool of potential employees, and were not dealing with significantly different complexities. Additionally, the restaurant with the better experience even managed to handle more customers with fewer staff members.

The answer lies in the environment created by leadership. The subtle yet profound impact of leadership on expectation and culture can influence every aspect of a business. It starts with the selection of specific qualities and values when hiring employees, which then shapes the overall culture and compounds over time.

Culture change is notoriously challenging because it permeates every facet of an organization. However, as a leader, you have the potential to create a positive impact. Begin by:

- Envisioning where you want your team or company to be.
- Identifying the changes or areas of focus that are essential to drive that impact.
- Working diligently to align your actions and expectations with those goals.

Effective leadership is not just about managing operations or making immediate decisions, it's also about creating an environment that fosters excellence and cultivates a thriving culture. This is the essence of leadership and where a leader holds the potential to make a lasting impact.

Leaders can fortify organizational worth by prioritizing people's growth and improvement through opportunities, goal setting, and acknowledgment. Boost the team's motivation by checking on them routinely (but with limited frequency) and providing feedback. When team members can easily communicate about their work, they can build greater trust in the leadership.

To create an organizational culture, a *leadership* culture is required. The way leaders communicate with each other and their team members is pivotal in the change process. This involves how they operate, make decisions, and interact. Leadership is about the daily work environment, beliefs, values, communication, and behaviors. The leader must understand their part in developing an organizational culture, and the organization should also consider the growth of its leaders.

Truly effective leadership is more than just adding to your organizational structure, training classes, or choosing the most suitable person while hiring the new leader. Producing modern leaders is the most efficient way to ensure your leadership culture serves the organizational culture. It is wise to consider the larger objective and the long-term strategy. And that's where the key importance of a leader's capabilities and ability to drive momentum within a team that the organization resides.

Leaders shape and carve out the organization's culture and help define the team's culture, goals, and direction. They have a huge effect on the culture of the company. A strong leader will provide their team with a purpose, a sense of vision, inspiration, and mentorship. The modern workforce's diversity is redefining the definition of success, both professionally and personally, and outdated leadership tactics are not resonating for maximum impact.

For instance, research says that only 54% of employees can ensure that their leaders know about their activities while at work (this gets even more complicated with remote employees). Roughly 26% think that their leader appreciates collaboration, and only around 59% believe their leader values their efforts (O. C. Tanner n.d.). Leaders' impact on organizational culture is tremendous, so their main focus should remain on their job, and inspiring people should be included in the leadership strategy.

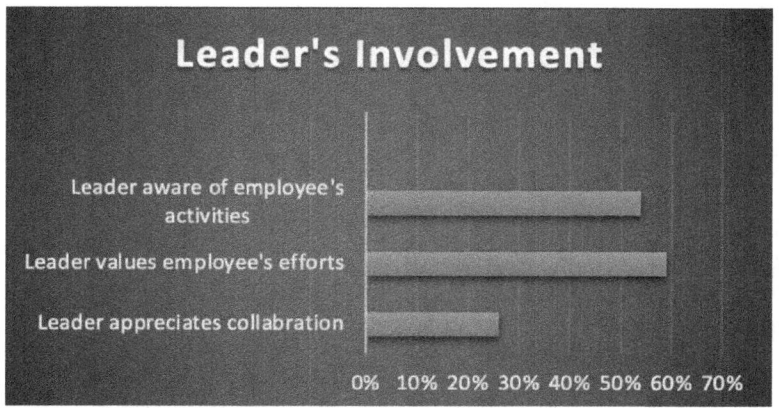

These statistics highlight a fundamental issue in the workplace—employees often feel undervalued and disconnected from their leaders. When a leader fails to appreciate collaboration or recognize the efforts of their team members, it can have a devastating impact on the morale of the entire organization. Employees who feel undervalued are more likely to become disengaged, which can lead to decreased productivity, high turnover rates, and even a toxic work environment.

Furthermore, with the rise of remote work, it is even more critical for leaders to establish trust and connection with their team members. When employees work remotely, it can be challenging to maintain a sense of belonging and engagement with the organization. Leaders who fail to adapt their leadership style to remote work can unintentionally create an environment of isolation and disconnection, leading to burnout and dissatisfaction among employees.

Therefore, leaders must prioritize inspiring and motivating their team members. When leaders make an effort to appreciate collaboration, value their employees' efforts, and maintain a strong connection with their team members they create a positive and productive work environment. And by doing so, leaders improve employee morale, engagement, and ultimately, the success of the organization as a whole.

Fostering a Positive Work Environment

Leaders drive collaboration between the team and know its importance in the long term. Sometimes observing the employees and their way of working can teach you about the working methods and the employee's behavior toward each other. It can be astonishing how much you can learn through observation while allowing space. Providing a safe space for employees to speak or ask about their concerns also helps in extraordinary ways. When employees feel their opinions are heard and valued, it boosts their morale and increases their sense of belonging as valued members of the organization.

To foster a positive work environment, leaders should also support their employees when they encounter failures. Remind them that failure is not the end but an opportunity to learn and grow. Despite one's best efforts, failure is inevitable, and maintaining a positive outlook and a willingness to learn from mistakes can lead to significant growth and development. This positive attitude can be passed on to the employees from the leader instead of punishing them for their mistakes. The organization's cultural strength is only as good as the leaders driving the initiatives.

Intentional Practicality: being purposeful in each action you make as a leader to influence an anticipated outcome for alignment with goals.

As a leader, every action you take has a ripple effect on the organization. Be intentional and purposeful in your approach, from the way you communicate to the decisions you make. This is where the concept of **Intentional Practicality** comes into play. The concept of **Intentional Practicality** builds on the need for purposeful action in each decision you make. Everything you do, say, or act upon affects a circumstance, so try to use that to your benefit for long-term strategy. Be authentic but use purposeful thought and intent with the *message* you are conveying.

Consider the traits people frequently attribute to great leaders: creative, smart, sympathetic, passionate, and visionary. However, something less obvious but quite as important is the attribute of intentionality. The intentional leader acts rather than reacts. The intentional leader understands how value is created and advances both the organization and his or her own goals through purposeful decisions, language, and actions. Align intentionality and practicality, and you will find the heart of the meaning of intentional practicality. One of the foundational elements behind the concept is the ability to make practical decisions.

Intentional decision example: *Specifically modeling a behavior to an employee.*

Potentially even setting up the scenario to positively reflect a modeled scenario.

Practical decision example: *setting a pattern or practice in place to purposefully build your teams capability overtime.*

As we dive deeper into the concept of Intentional Practicality, it becomes clear that intentional leaders employ a variety of practices to set themselves apart and achieve long-term success. Here are a few of the important areas they employ:

THEY ARE DELIBERATE ABOUT WHAT THEY STAND FOR

Whether or not a leader intentionally develops a "leadership brand," they do so by displaying the value they provide, the results they achieve, and how this is communicated to stakeholders. Even though you may not have considered it to be building a leadership brand, you may be doing this already.

You can carve out your unique value proposition as a leader if you have contributed a particular skill or talent to the solution of a larger problem or to the advancement of the organization.

THEY PLAN TO DELIVER ON WHAT THEY STAND FOR

What do leaders do with their time? Where do they put their efforts? What proficient improvement will they embrace to fortify their authority image?

It's easy to let demands from customers, employees, and other external factors dictate priorities every day. Every leader must, without a doubt, respond, but they also manage their time to keep plans and priorities on track.

THEY ARE SELF-AWARE

They know that every part of their behavior is examined to see if it matches their leadership brand. They communicate with their teams, customers, and peers through their words, actions, decisions, and to some extent, their appearance.

If you are a leader, you may have heard the expression, "You set the weather in the office every day." Your team will sense if you are cheerful and optimistic. The team's mood will also decline if you are clearly downtrodden. This is something the intentional leader acknowledges and takes advantage of.

THEY SET LEADERSHIP MILESTONES

They set milestones (*milestones represent a significant event or achievement in the project*) and never quit attempting to accomplish them. It's helpful to distinguish leadership milestones from objectives. There are numerous types of objectives for leaders: financial, customer contentment, employee engagement, and more. Milestones go beyond specific business performance or results and give an analytical way to represent goals.

Leaders can be found in many different areas of an organization – and it isn't just a single leader at the top of the organization driving everything. In any given organization you can find a wide array of leaders in many different capacities, such as traditional leaders, managers, vice presidents, CEOs, and non-traditional leaders (*leaders on a team that are individual contributors, an individual that the team refers to and values their guidance and feedback heavily – but may not have the official title*). Leadership is not simply a *title* per se but more of a *designation*.

Culture, Communication, and The Leader

A company without a clearly defined or well-understood culture or mission will fail in the long run. Most of the time, the reason for this is a leader's poor communication because they prioritize profit over the efforts and well-being of the employee. This develops unhealthy competition, a bullying culture among the staff, and micromanagement. Moreover, a weak culture increases absenteeism and low engagement. Team members start lacking empathy and flexibility and become disloyal towards the goal, whereas a healthy workplace helps build up the team with the right resources.

Company culture helps measure organizational success. Strategically bringing change to the organization's culture requires a determined and disciplined leader who will make the organization their main priority. Good organizational culture contributes to employee well-being and motivates them to work harder, better, and stronger together.

Additional Thoughts

The culture of a company is greatly influenced by its leaders. They manage, lead, set the agenda, prioritize work, and delegate appropriately. The people they lead benefit from strong leaders' vision, a sense of purpose, mentorship, and motivation.

The definition of personal and professional success is changing as a result of today's diverse workforce. Younger generations, who value more growth and coaching, are not responding well to traditional leadership styles or leadership culture (which leaves a gap for improvement opportunities for us to fill).

A positive, productive culture that encourages employee engagement and drives business success can be established by leaders who display intentional practicality. However, when leaders are ineffective, they may unintentionally create a hostile work environment that results in employee dissatisfaction and the decline of the organization.

Leaders must be aware of their influence on organizational culture and ensure that they are cultivating a culture that is in line with the company's objectives and values. They can accomplish this by fostering an atmosphere at work that encourages employees to participate and make contributions.

The shared beliefs, values, or perceptions carried by employees within an organization can be referred to as organizational culture. We find that leaders are the driving forces in their early development because we are aware that a shared mindset is the foundation of organizational culture.

The organization's members learn and pass on culture as a collective. Your leaders are the ones who initially determine which values are absorbed and passed on. They decide what the organization should and shouldn't do, as well as its ethics and beliefs.

A strong organizational culture emerges once these core values are established, and employees recognize and uphold them.

Chapter 4

Recruiting and Retaining

Most organizations know the value of goal setting, but that should not be the only point of focus. Individual goals must also align with team and organizational goals so everyone is moving in the same direction.

Aligning goals creates a unified working environment where everyone is aware of their specific role. If your organizational goals are not aligned with the employees, you are at a disadvantage.

Proper alignment differentiates between a high performing and a low-performing team or company. Research done by LSA Global tells that highly aligned companies generate 58% faster revenue, are also 78% more profitable, and perform better than unaligned peers in customer satisfaction and retainment, employee engagement, and leadership. (Kristin Ryba - Quantum Workplace 2021)

Goals set the tone of organizational strategy, amplifying what's important and making it easier for employees to work according to those standards. Breaking down organizational goals into smaller, achievable milestones can help create a roadmap for success, providing employees with clear markers along the way and ultimately contributing to the achievement of the company's overall strategic objectives.

Goal alignment can help prevent employees from feeling lost - it's common to stop understanding the point of their efforts over time if they are not aligned for their roles. When they are well aware of their functional purpose on the team, it will provide them with a better sense of how their work is contributing to the organizational goals. It will increase accountability and provide meaning and purpose in their work.

In many cases, priorities will be evident. When you can align the effects of each task to the organizational goal(s), people can more easily conceptualize and procedurally process what should be done first. This will actively encourage everyone to work in synchronicity because they are now on the same page.

Employees tend to get demotivated (discouraged, lose ambition, and lose interest) when they feel like they are working alone. But understanding how each person's efforts can complement the organizational goal(s) and can create a strong bond for each team member. It is important in long-term decision-making strategies to align the team members with the culture and the strategy of the larger team/organization.

The capacity of an organization to maximize and optimize its workforce as well as their cognitive abilities, such as the courage and confidence to commit to the strategy, are critical to the success of a long-term strategy. Each of the following are key factors that lead to that ability:

- **Humility** to be **trustworthy**, **receptive** to new knowledge, and **supportive** through well-reasoned guidance.
- **Discipline** to carry out the **plan** and to adhere to it.
- Capacity to **communicate clearly, precisely,** and **promptly**.

Leaders can establish a vision for the future, outline measurable goals, maximize collaborative and relational opportunities, and align teams by planning well in advance. In addition to providing direction for day-to-day decision-making, strategic planning provides a blueprint for the growth of an organization. Assessing progress and promoting a culture of continuous learning can help businesses develop their cycles and frameworks.

Creating a high-performance team means hiring the right people for the role. This isn't just about choosing people with a range of abilities. It is also about choosing people who can work well together.

A successful high-performing team encompasses people who are highly skilled and willing to align their primary focus toward achieving a common goal. The team is assigned the same goal for which they must work together as a whole with a shared vision and values. This cohesiveness produces trust and builds a united organization.

Myths in beliefs...

During the early stages of my career in a leadership role, I held a misguided belief that a "great manager" could take any group of employees, regardless of their skills or capabilities, and transform them into a high-performing all-star team. However, I soon learned from a wise manager that while it may be theoretically possible, it is not very likely to be achievable. The key lies in having the right people for the job.

Let's consider the analogy of a bathroom remodel. Imagine you are tasked with completing the project, but you are given a roofer and a carpenter. While both individuals can technically "do the job", they lack the specific expertise required specifically for a bathroom remodel. As a result, the project may take longer than expected, exceed the budget, and even when it is eventually completed, it may not meet the necessary standards. The job could still get done and may turn out great but having someone with the experience, skills, knowledge, and expertise would benefit many other aspects of the intended outcome.

This example highlights the importance of building a team with individuals who possess the appropriate knowledge and skills for their respective roles. To ensure successful outcomes, you must surround yourself with highly skilled people who possess expertise in their respective areas and often who surpass your own capabilities.

Not Paying Attention to Team Size: A Common Mistake

When creating a team, there will be numerous challenges to face, but an easy one to control is the size of the team. There is only a certain amount of efficient results a given number of individuals can produce within a team. After a certain point, communication breakdowns and process separation can become unmanageable and leads to a slowdown in effectiveness. Gathering a multitude of members may seem like a viable solution in the short term, but can ultimately affect productivity, cause poor coordination, and increase stress levels. Workers in teams depend on each other to complete tasks, and the larger the team gets, the harder it will be for the combined feedback loop to expand. This causes more incomplete work in the end, which will affect the goal or goals.

On the basketball court, teams have five players, football teams have eleven players, and bridge teams have two players. When it comes to team size in business, there are no hard and fast rules like in sports. But there are established standards that have proven successful in the past. Generally, projects with teams of five to eight individuals have shown the most success. This size fits the standard pattern seen in many innovative and decentralized start-ups that have grown into successful businesses. Most management experts agree that a group of five to nine people is ideal. This is due to the focus of research studies on processes and outcomes, highlighting the significant impact that team size can have on overall success. If the team has too few members, it may not have enough resources or skills. When there are too many people, communication becomes more difficult.

In one study, Dr. Meredith Belbin conducted extensive research on teams in the U.K. prior to 1990. She found that the ideal team size was eight, along with one specialist as needed (Boundless 2016). When there were fewer than five members, there were few perspectives and less creativity. With more than twelve members, there was more conflict and a greater chance that subgroups would form, which could break up the team's unity.

According to research, additional factors that affect the optimal team size include:

- The specific problem domain for the job or task the team will be working on.
- The skills needed to complete the job successfully.
- The amount of time required to complete the work.

The answers to those questions frequently determine the best team size. If the task is a sales function, for instance, one person may complete most of the work until the finance and delivery/inventory manager gets involved. It may be ideal for one company to have four employees with multiple skill sets. In contrast, another company may need six or seven employees to achieve the same abilities. Lastly, the team may have fewer members and shorter flex points for the tasks' completion time.

Identifying and effectively utilizing diverse opportunities can also prove to be beneficial while building a team. In recent years, there has been much more of a corporate focus on creating a team with diversity in areas such as creativity, objectivity, and thought. Don't neglect the opportunity to pay attention to each team member and potential new employees' life experiences and stories because the most creative ideas come from a diverse team. Often, the benefits of someone's diverse perspective aren't apparent in initial conversations.

Benefits of Emotional Intelligence

Therefore, life experiences and different backgrounds bring unique ideas to the table. Another critical point to identify in candidates while hiring is their emotional intelligence, which encompasses their ability to handle conflict, stress, their level of self-awareness, and their ability to be empathetic toward others. Emotional intelligence is a crucial skill for any employee to possess, especially in a team setting. Individuals who have a high level of emotional intelligence can handle conflicts and other stressful situations in a more effective and constructive way. They can empathize with their team members and can communicate their own emotions clearly and respectfully. In a team, emotional intelligence can lead to better collaboration, improved relationships, and increased productivity.

5 Essential Factors When Hiring and Recruiting

EXPERIENCE

THE RESULT OF CONFIDENCE AND KNOWLEDGE COMBINED.

Experience gives team members the ability to be aware of the problems and how to solve them because they will have been in similar situations prior. This will improve the work and hasten overall performance.

For example, when hiring engineers, experience is a significant factor to consider. Candidates who have demonstrated success in similar positions are likely to be able to do so at your company. To make an objective assessment, evaluate the level of success achieved in the past.

POTENTIAL

When conducting interviews, you might come across candidates who appear promising but don't have a great deal of experience. They might be a recent college graduate or someone with only a few years directly in the field. This is where you will need to evaluate the candidate at a deeper level for the potential. Each candidate is an investment, some may take much more of an upfront investment of trust but have potential to pay dividends in the long term. This can be a bit of a subjective task because you have to anticipate their demonstratable skills within a short introductory session.

Companies and teams of all sizes make mistakes. Hiring and promoting new growth is a strong indicator that the company is trying to improve in a particular area. Focus on key comments from the candidate and see what areas of interest ignite excitement for the candidate and what they are truly passionate about. Identify areas of potential they could organically grow in due to their stated passion(s).

As a leader, you may decide to take a chance on less experienced candidates from time to time. For instance, conducting interviews with engineers who recently graduated at the top of their class. Although these candidates have not yet demonstrated themselves in the professional work environment, their potential may be evident. These candidates may develop into outstanding employees on your team.

Culture Fit

It always helps to consider how a given candidate will match up with the company's current culture. Enjoyment at work contributes to a decrease in employee turnover when employees are a team and cultural fit. During interviews, be sure to ask appropriate questions to get a good understanding of how the candidate will fit with the existing team.

The culture of each business is unique and serves as a driving factor for the business and its employees. Some businesses, for instance, may encourage employees to regularly work late to complete tasks basis (which can serve as a detractor to their culture over time). While in other companies, employees may be highly encouraged or even required to leave on time to ensure their work/life balance is well distributed. Cultivating a healthy culture may seem to be at odds with pursuing progress, but making that difficult decision, which may be harder in the short term, tends to pay off in the long term. People first, then Process.

Hard Skills

Hard skills are measurable and simple-to-define abilities that candidates have acquired through previous employment or education—tangible experience. When hiring for an advanced position that requires a domain of understanding specific to the field, hard skills can't be overlooked. Candidates won't be able to do the job without training if they don't have the right skills. Investing in that additional training can be costly and may have additional upfront and long-term costs that may not be immediately evident.

If you were looking to hire a civil engineer, you would want someone familiar with the proprietary tools of the trade and an aptitude for utilizing appropriate tools, services, and/or hardware or software specific to the trade. Candidates who do not possess those hard skills will have a difficult time performing and being successful at the job. They shouldn't be considered a good fit, as it would result in a misalignment of the position.

SOFT SKILLS

Even though hard skills are important, you can't afford to neglect soft skills. Soft skills are difficult to measure and frequently (and somewhat erroneously) considered *personality traits*. Soft skills, for instance, include the ability to communicate effectively, a strong work ethic, and working well with the team.

Candidates may possess impressive hard skills but will not succeed on your team if they lack the appropriate soft skills. This is a consideration that should be evaluated with a great deal of importance in all candidates. Soft skills are intangible skills that are hard to "teach" to some and can be costly to the team if overlooked.

Some essential soft skills that could leave an impact:

- **Flexibility and Adaptability**: People who are flexible and adaptable are able to keep up and change with the times. They are also able to take on new challenges and learn new skills quickly.
- **Conflict resolution**: Conflict resolution is the ability to resolve conflicts quickly and efficiently—not giving in or giving up easily but finding a way to ensure the best outcome with the least resistance. People who are good at conflict resolution can stay calm under pressure and see both sides of a situation. They are also able to find innovative solutions to problems and untangle difficult situations.
- **Collaboration**: People who are good at collaborating or have communication skills work well with others and build strong relationships easily.

These team players are able to compromise, see things from other people's perspectives, be objective, and exercise strong verbal communication.

A person's "soft skills" are a set of positive qualities and skills that can make them more marketable in the workplace, improve relationships, and boost productivity and performance at work. Other soft skills include communication and active listening, building and maintaining positive relationships, collaboration and cooperation, civility, and being open and objective to feedback.

Successful businesses know the value of hiring the right people. This is why companies spend an average of $3,300 per hire—so they can have the right person onboard. In the United States alone, $72 billion a year is invested in recruiting and hiring. But even after putting time, energy, and money into searching for the right employee, mistakes are inevitable and cost a lot. (Olsen n.d.)

Hiring the wrong person can cost a considerable amount of time, effort, and money to the company. Harvard Business Review estimated that 80% of turnover results from poor hiring decisions. Replacing an employee statistically costs approximately one-third of their salary, so those numbers ascend quickly. But the damage from misaligned hiring is more than turnover costs. Costs are also linked with decreased work production, disruptive company culture, and future loss of customers and revenue.

This is precisely why making the right hiring choices are essential in building and creating a successful company. Despite knowing the value of making the right decisions when hiring, it's still easy to make mistakes (we are dealing with humans, after all). Often, it comes down to a subjective judgment call and alignment with perceived skills. By staying cautious of the risks and following practical steps, companies can avoid bad hiring choices while saving money and time for the future.

Moving from a *good-enough* company to an *excellent* company requires disciplined people, disciplined processes, highly engaged action, adequate goal setting, deep communication/collaboration, and well-planned thought. Finding and aligning *disciplined people* means consistently adding employees that are *right* for the organization.

The concept of "First Who, Then What" (Collins, First who, Then what... n.d.) is pioneered in Jim Collins's book *Good to Great*, and is based on disciplined people. It involves the leader being great but also sheds light on the importance of the quality of each team member. This concept suggests taking an approach contrary to our usual rational thinking. It means that you don't first need to decide what you want to do and then look for the people you need for it. Instead, start by hiring the right people and eliminating the wrong ones from the organization. The level of importance on this topic is pivotal to the overall goals and missions, not only for the organization but also for the immediate team.

Searching for and identifying the right people can sometimes be more important than vision, strategy, and almost everything else in the mix. The primary concern tends to be to hire the right candidate for the role and then working on aiming toward the target or goal. On the other end of the spectrum, the negative effect that occurs when hiring the wrong person spills over into a multitude of problems and increases with time. Not to mention, multiple misaligned people can completely change the company culture negatively. The *first who, then what* concept is all about changing your idea about the importance of people and molding it to the importance of the *right* people.

By first prioritizing "who" over "what", teams can more easily pivot in a different direction. This is because their loyalty lies with the people they work with rather than the specific tasks they are working on. This concept highlights the importance of focusing on the right people within an organization to achieve sustained success. Secondly, you will save time by motivating the team members as they will be more inclined to be self-motivated. Third, this approach provides the company with an opportunity to strive for greatness by ensuring only the right people are in leadership positions, further emphasizing the importance of putting *who* before *what*.

First who, then what also includes three important principles and one of the essential principles is: When in doubt, don't hire; keep looking. Top companies are only willing to grow on the condition of hiring the right people.

In the *first who* principle: *It is not how you compensate your executives. It is which executives you have to reimburse first.* If you have the right members on the team, they will aim to do whatever they can to create a great company, not because of what they will "achieve" for it, but because they cannot imagine settling for anything less. Their values require building excellence for its own sake, and you are no more likely to change that with a compensation package than you are likely to affect whether they breathe. Good companies understand a simple truth: The right people will aim to do the right things and produce the best results they are capable of, regardless of the incentive system.

Principle number two states: When you know you need to make a change in personnel, act right away. Let go of the misaligned personnel. It is unfair to them, the team, and the organization to keep them on board.

Once you know you need to make a personnel change, be diligent in the decision but not ruthless in the implementation. Instead, help people exit with dignity and grace so that later, the majority of people who have exited continue to have a positive outlook about your organization. Regardless of any hiring mistakes, systematically apply lessons learned to future hiring decisions.

Principle three: Put your best people on your most significant opportunities. This can serve as rocket fuel to drive progress within the organization. This is where the potential for scalability arises; it also empowers productivity.

When challenged with any opportunity or critical situation, switch the decision from "what" (*what should we do?*) to "who" (*who would be the right person to take responsibility?*). Spend a significant portion of time on people decisions: get the right people aligned with the proper tasks, coordinate those people in the right places, shift the wrong people (*in the sense of wrong for the effort, not the organization*) away from the wrong tasks, develop people so they can handle bigger opportunities, and plan for succession. Develop a disciplined, systematic process for getting the right people coordinated for the proper tasks and goals.

Once you fill your segments of planned work with the right people in alignment with the right goals, it becomes less of a question of where you're headed; instead, it becomes how far you can go.

You can create a *good* organization by managing problems but utilizing opportunities will make you great. So, it is best to put the most capable people at the front so that they create or handle the biggest opportunities. Some of the most effective ways to ensure you are doing so include:

Initiate new ideas

Be proactive and develop new concepts. While creative thinking may be out of your comfort zone, you will develop more possibilities, learn a lot, and inspire others.

Pay attention to what your coworkers say (*above and below you*)

Being a good listener and applying active listening skills demonstrates that you are truly interested in your colleagues. Active listening skills enhance workplace performance. Additionally, it helps demonstrate a caring and compassionate attitude and reduces misunderstandings, which leads to a higher likelihood that tasks will be accomplished on time.

Go the extra mile

Take initiative to complete tasks without being reminded. Your team will take notice over time. Doing more than what is expected or required can result in higher expectations for the team while providing a path for others to follow your lead.

Applying these principles will help you make the right hiring decisions. With the right employees, everyone will be more engaged in the workplace. Meetings will be less daunting and more interesting, which will help build great organic relationships between the team.

A great deal of influence lies in the hands of the employees, so leaders must focus on maintaining a healthy, engaged workforce. As difficult as it is to earn an employee's loyalty, it is essential to business success. As mentioned, an average employee exit costs 33% of their annual salary (Li 2022). It costs a considerable amount of money, effort, and realignment to replace an employee.

To secure a strong and capable team, it is imperative to invest time and resources in the recruitment process. This involves advertising for the right candidates, screening their qualifications, conducting thorough interviews, and selecting the best candidate for the job. The cost of employee turnover can be significant, not just in terms of lost talent and time, but also in terms of financial resources and valuable domain expertise. Therefore, it is crucial to prioritize hiring the right employees and retaining them by providing an inclusive work environment, opportunities for growth, and recognition of their contributions. In doing so, the company can reap the benefits of a talented, loyal, and dedicated workforce.

Lack of proper management skills makes employees 4x closer to quitting.[12] Take a moment, and really think through the opportunity about how detrimental of an impact that can have to the organization—especially at scale.

Managers not focused on the primary goal of being a great leader while setting a high standard can negatively affect employees and result in high turnover, even for the best employees. According to TINNY pulse data, 21% of employees start hunting for another job when they don't feel recognized, compared to only 12.4% of those otherwise.

Employees need validation for their work and stay more loyal when appreciated.[12]

Providing employees with validation is one of the best ways to improve relationships in the organization. Employees working must establish a value for the goal, develop a positive attitude, and manage any feeling of isolation. When employees are appreciated for their work, their productivity increases, and they become more trustworthy, cooperative, and loyal. But when employees don't feel important in an organization, their interest in the goal fades.

Relying on outdated recruitment methods just because they have worked in the past is a common misconception that can lead to poor hiring decisions. What worked in the past may not be effective now, you must be open to new strategies for finding the right candidates. Otherwise, you may be limiting the potential for achieving quality and diversity in hiring. Not only can it lead to overlooking qualified candidates, but it can also result in a slower and less efficient hiring process.

Although interviews are not easy to conduct, they can reveal a lot of information about the candidate beyond their resume. When conducting thorough interviews, you can find out how the candidate has handled difficult situations in the past and elaborate on their personal experiences and skills.

ADDITIONAL THOUGHTS

When searching for new employees to expand teams in a business, it is crucial to have a formal hiring procedure in place. Hiring the right people is crucial to your company's success. In doing so it will ensure the longevity of your company and team success. This will increase your chances of recruiting the best candidates and avoiding costly and painful mistakes. If you invest the effort and time to find the right people, the anticipated outcome of goals will be more likely to succeed.

Great leaders can identify the right fit for the job while hiring. However, solely relying on your gut is insufficient in this decision. It is important to ensure what skill-set they can provide and whether the candidate will possess the aptitude to align with the organizational culture.

Hiring the wrong person for a critical position not only results in a major hassle but can also lead to unnecessary expenditure of valuable resources like time and money in the hiring process. Allowing the wrong person to occupy the position for an extended period can lead to significant issues for your company.

These threats are especially risky for teams and organizations where new hires frequently play a crucial role in establishing the culture of the company in the future.

Communication and administration become more complicated when there are more people involved, which means your estimated efforts will also need to expand or scale to suit. Layers of unnecessary complication produce extra debt to the team and overall organization.

Soft skills are related to emotional intelligence. Employees with emotional intelligence and the ability to work in teams and communicate effectively are in high demand among employers. The soft skills required in a workplace include:

Leadership skills: Employers are looking for workers who can lead and supervise other employees. They are looking for people who can build relationships at all company levels. Building teams, resolving conflicts, and cultivating the desired culture are all responsibilities of leaders.

One essential aspect of leadership is influencing others and meeting their needs. Far too many businesses overlook it when placing someone with the most technical expertise in a position of authority. The development of soft skills is frequently a crucial component of leadership training and can often be one of the most difficult.

Teamwork: Most employees are part of a team, a department, or a division, and even those not officially on a team need to work together. You might prefer to work independently, but it's essential to collaborate with others to achieve the company's objective—demonstrating that you have the soft skills needed to collaborate effectively.

Communication Skills: There are five components to effective communication. The ability to communicate clearly and briefly verbally is known as verbal communication. Conveying enough, but not too much can be a delicate balance. It's important when conveying details to not overload people with too much information, while also providing them enough pertinent information to convey the requirements.

In addition to having a sharpened capability for conveying your message, it is also important to project positive body language and facial expressions. Your body language and nonverbal communication can accompany or derail a conversation.

Enabling you to openly listen and hear what others are saying, known as active listening, should also be considered a crucial soft skill in communication. To communicate effectively with someone, you must be able to listen. Any attempts at communication will likely be one-sided and ineffective if you do not have strong listening skills.

Problem-Solving Skills: Misunderstandings, issues, and roadblocks are all part of the job and serve as learning opportunities. Demonstrating the ability to truly rationalize and objectively step through utilizing problem-solving skills can help in any avenue of your career and excel in it when you apply your knowledge to solve pressing issues and develop viable solutions.

Work Ethic: Companies don't like to spend time micromanaging employees (and rightfully so), it's demanding of time and resources, it's detrimental to moral, and it is effectively a loss of productivity. They expect you to be responsible and perform the work for which you are paid, which includes arriving on time, meeting deadlines, and producing minimal error work.

Flexibility/Adaptability: Businesses need to make quick (and sometimes drastic) changes. As a result, they are looking for employees who can also change gears or directions as needed. Now more than ever, employees need to handle various tasks and demonstrate a willingness to take on responsibilities that may fall outside of their area of expertise as organizations have become more self-led and less hierarchical over the past decade.

Interpersonal Skills: Interpersonal skill is a broad category of "Personal Skills", including using diplomacy, developing rapport, and maintaining relationships.

Chapter 5

Game Theory

Game theory is the study of cooperative and noncooperative strategies for games and social situations in which players must choose between individual and collective benefits. That being said, there are practical use cases in modern business. Participants in Game Theory scenarios must make decisions that have an impact not only on themselves but on other participants as well. The major central themes surrounding the concepts of Game Theory are:

- **Strategic Interactions**: Game theory primarily deals with strategic interactions where the outcomes for each participant depend not only on their actions, but also on the actions of the others involved.

- **Rationality**: Game theory assumes that individuals involved are rational decision-makers. This means they make choices that maximize their expected utility, taking into account their preferences and beliefs.

- **Equilibrium**: Equilibrium concepts are fundamental in game theory. These include Nash equilibrium (*where no player has an incentive to change their strategy*) and subgame perfect equilibrium (*a refinement of Nash equilibrium for sequential games*). Equilibrium solutions help forecast how rational players might behave.

- **Cooperation and Competition**: Game theory explores the balance between cooperation (*working together for mutual benefit*) and competition (*pursuing individual gain*) in various situations. It often examines how cooperative outcomes can be sustained and why competition can lead to suboptimal results that are not desirable.

Embedded in Game Theory is the study of how strategic interactions between participants can affect the outcome of a situation and translates to modern business. By analyzing the actions and reactions of competitors, companies can better understand how to position their own products and services for success, making Game Theory an essential tool for strategic decision-making. It is a technique for examining how companies, governments, and people should respond to strategic situations where they need to communicate with each other. In determining what to do, they have to focus on what others will probably do and how they might respond to current situations.

When applied to more complex games with more than two decision-makers, Game Theory becomes more speculative because of the inherent depth of complexities of these games. It is challenging to monitor and describe rational behavior in these scenarios because decision-makers are confronted with forces they cannot control, however, it proves as a great model for hypothesizing business interactions.

Game Theory has been used to study concepts as fundamental as card games while it has also been used to study human and institutional behavior, which has led to large strides forward in social sciences. Game Theory models are utilized in a vast range of fields including sociology, computer science, economics, politics, psychology, mathematics, and philosophy.

Even though Game Theory has roots that go back to ancient times and the 18th century, it has only been recognized as a scientific field in the early 20th century when researchers tried to use quantitative analysis to solve abstract cognitive problems. During the early years of the Cold War, significant advancements were made in Game Theory that established it as a scientific discipline with measurable proof. Consequently, economic and pricing strategies, war games and global military strategy, social issues, and even labor bargaining all benefited from Game Theory applications.

With Game Theory in your arsenal, you'll be equipped to make strategic moves that give you an edge over your competitors.

When I think about Game Theory in its purest format, I can't help but think about the concepts/constructs around the game of chess. Each move has the potential to affect each subsequent move, requiring a deep level of thinking past the immediate play – this is where strategic thinking/planning comes into play. Depending on your degree of cognitive complexity, you may be able to think a few moves ahead or potentially a multitude of moves along, but the other challenge here is 'knowing your opponent'. This is a crucial factor because you must be able to simultaneously plan your moves while anticipating your opponent's next moves, all while adjusting to the actual plays being made.

Just like in Game Theory, everyone *in play* has the opportunity to be utilized for the *result* you are *planning*. The concepts shouldn't be used recklessly, as there is a great degree of potential to end up much like a falling house of cards. When you are molding your strategic thinking to think past your immediate results, it tends to require meticulously thinking ahead to ensure the intended outcome for the adjustments required to land with the intended outcome expected. This requires planning, and knowing *your opponent*.

On the other side of this, psychology plays a significant role in influencing others to get the desired result. You need to know what each one of the player's values are so you can utilize that in their/your favor for the anticipated outcome required. When utilizing these concepts in a team it needs to be utilized with a win/win scenario in mind. The trick here is to strike a valuable incentive balance for all player outcomes. It's important to remember, you are *influencing* people or *guiding* them, and this leaves a lot of volatility for misuse. So use the concepts wisely and make sure you are considering the impacts, not only for yourself but the other parties involved also. When used wisely the resulting outcomes can produce highly beneficial results. However, on the other end of the spectrum, misuse will almost guarantee ultimately ending up in a tailspin spiraling towards detrimental outcome.

To a certain degree, the concepts surrounding Game Theory tend to have a variance to be misunderstood and potentially mis-utilized when applied incorrectly, this can play out as just using/manipulating people. When mis-utilized for selfish gain, the effect will inevitably only produce short-term results (*normally crashing down like a house of cards*). But when used wisely and effectively, the effects can be a beautiful orchestration of coordinated outcomes benefiting all parties.

Game Theory is also useful in business for modeling the competing actions of economic agents. Businesses are frequently required to make several strategic decisions that affect their ability to make money. They may be faced with dilemmas such as deciding whether to create new products, develop old ones, or employ new marketing strategies.

Businesses have the option of selecting their rival. Some compete with other market participants and focus on external forces, while others strive to be better than their previous versions and set internal goals. Whether internal or external, companies are constantly at odds for resources, attempting to hire the best candidates away from competition, and attract customers away from competing products.

Game Theory can be used as a strategic tool in times of uncertainty because it provides perspectives on how players might behave in various situations and offer additional helpful information for decision-making. According to Adam M. Brandenburger and Barry J. Nalebuff, authors of the book *Coopetition*, the primary use of Game Theory for business is to help decision-makers determine when to cooperate and when to compete. (Brandenburger 1996)

Managerial decisions and strategies are based on a multitude of factors, such as a leader's prediction of a competitor's actions and prepared responses to those actions. Game theory provides an analytical framework for interpreting the course of action most *likely* to produce the desired outcomes.

Leaders benefit from this kind of preparation by being able to make well-informed decisions during events ranging from product launches and pricing to choosing a target market and marketing campaigns. The idea of "securing a competitive advantage" involves, in a way, applying Game Theory.

In business decision-making, Game Theory addresses more than just a straightforward two-fold relationship between two rivals' actions. In any industry, there is often a great deal of competition (opponents). A competitor's every move has the potential to initiate a long-term reaction and event chain.

In addition, a successful growth strategy for a business frequently entails a one-of-a-kind combination of stability, creativity, and (sometimes) disruption. On the other hand, risk assessments and cost-versus-benefit analyses are necessary for predicting the effects that innovation and disruption will have on a business.

Business leaders, like chess players, use Game Theory to plan for various scenarios and anticipate numerous "moves". As required, they prepare for rapid, preplanned strategy iterations. In times of disruption and uncertainty, this anticipation can help businesses expand while remaining competitive and adaptable.

Every strategic game has players, a scenario, and strategic choices that can be made. Beyond that, there are all the possible outcomes and payoffs for each option. To help illustrate the opportunity it presents toward better critical thinking in business, I'll offer several practical Game Theory games and their applications.

THE CENTIPEDE GAME

In the centipede game, two players must decide whether to take or leave a sum that increases with each turn. The players must trust each other in this game and keep passing the sum to improve it. At the end of the game, they will each receive the most significant sum possible. Each player will receive less than if they cooperated if one player takes the sum before the game ends. This concept has been made popular through many mainstream TV game shows such as: *Deal or No Deal.* In business, this game creates a situation where two entities, possibly rival businesses, must trust each other. To achieve the greatest possible outcome for everyone, in the long run, the best strategy requires them to disregard their present self-interest.

THE DICTATOR GAME

In this Game Theory scenario, a sum of money is split between two players. The second player cannot influence the first player's choice, but they must divide a certain amount of cash with the first player. This creates a situation where one party has access to information that another party does not. Both players get to keep their respective portions of the cash if the second player accepts the first player's proposed division. However, if they reject it, neither party benefits. This scenario presents another example of how different businesses or individuals working together in a company can collaborate to achieve the best possible outcome for both parties.

THE PRISONER'S DILEMMA

Although the name may sound a bit unconventional, this game provides excellent scenarios to aid in strategic business decisions. In this game, you take two individual prisoners (or *players* for modeling the concepts aligning with Game Theory), separate them, and ask them to confess to a crime they may have committed together in this game. There are four possible outcomes: either both parties can confess, they can both blame each other, only one party can confess, or neither party can. Players in this game are expected to act strategically out of self-interest leading to a less-than-ideal outcome for both parties. In business, this is applied to a situation where two businesses offer products at odds with one another. If one company raises prices to gain an advantage over the competition, the other company will have to do the same, lowering both companies' maximum profits.

You may have picked up on the common theme of relying on self-interest as a motivator. The benefit of self-interest works with certain problem scenarios better than others, and similarly better audiences than others—so know your audience and understand your situation well beforehand. While it's important to understand your audience and situation well before relying on self-interest as a motivator, there are drawbacks to this approach. In a team setting, acting out of self-interest can lead to a breakdown in collaboration and hinder progress toward shared goals. Instead, prioritizing the interests of the team can foster a sense of unity and cooperation, ultimately leading to greater success. By putting the team's goals above individual interests, team members can work together more effectively and achieve more than they could on their own.

Now, let's move to some real-world applications of Game Theory to help us break it down it more common contexts.

Bidding At Auction

An auction is a sale in which multiple bidders compete to purchase a good or service, and the item is then sold to the highest bidder. In bid auctions, Game Theory is used, particularly for analyzing sealed auction bidding at the first price. Bids must be submitted securely and locked in this kind of auction.

Despite having complete information, the various players attempt to devise a bidding strategy, despite not knowing the value of each other's goods or services. During bid preparation, decisions are made based on bidders' behavior and other factors.

COLLECTIVE BARGAINING OR NEGOTIATION BETWEEN PARTIES

Different collective bargaining or negotiation activities between various parties or participants involve Game Theory. During a strike or lockout, worker unions and management engage in negotiations to raise wages. With the use of Game Theory, both parties can determine the best approach to solving the problem, such as considering different options for salaries and benefits that can benefit workers and management the most. Salary negotiation is another example where Game Theory can be applied. Purchasing negotiations with suppliers, compensation or incentive negotiations between management and suppliers, and even business partners often employ Game Theory elements to achieve the best outcome. Game Theory offers a useful framework for understanding and optimizing negotiation outcomes for all involved parties.

DECISIONS RELATED TO NEW PRODUCTS

Businesses use Game Theory to make decisions based on a product, such as whether to launch a new product or exit the launch. Businesses can utilize concepts from Game Theory to determine whether there is a first-mover advantage, what competitors might do with new products, and what defense tactics or strategies to use. Game Theory is also used to decide whether to enter or exit a new market.

PRODUCT PRICING DECISIONS

Customers' and retailers' pricing strategies are heavily influenced by Game Theory applications. Offering attractive discounts on goods to increase sales of complementary products is one-way retailers compete with one another to gain market share. For instance, garment shop vendors or retailers offer attractive deals on a particular stock of clothes during the offseason (a.k.a. "off-summer" or "off-winter" season), employing optimal pricing strategies to attract maximum customers. With this, retailers use a Game Theory strategy in which consumers and retailers are the primary players. While consumers prefer to select the best deal regarding discount and variety, retailers focus on employing the most effective pricing strategy.

STOCK MARKET DECISIONS

The stock market's buying and selling decisions can be made wisely using Game Theory. Investors make various stock market decisions using multiple investment strategies and considering different players or investors. The concepts around Game Theory make it possible to anticipate other players' decisions regarding investments. Based on these predictions, players can choose strategies for themselves that can result in tremendous profit.

Putting it All Together: Game Theory for Team Benefit

Now, lets step back to that same initial question of: how do we use this to apply to a team paradigm instead of self-interest? The theoretical concepts constructed around Game Theory can be applied constructively to a team paradigm by encouraging team members to focus not only on their own self-interests but also on those of the team as a whole. By understanding different strategies and outcomes that can arise from various decisions, team members can work together to achieve a mutually beneficial outcome.

Learning about the Game Theory concepts that use self-interest as a motivator provides a framework for understanding how people make decisions in situations where they have conflicting interests. However, it is equally important to recognize that in a team setting, individual self-interests may not always align with the interests of the team. This is where responsible application of Game Theory concepts comes into play.

Team members should approach problem-solving and decision-making with a mindset of cooperation and collaboration, seeking solutions that benefit everyone rather than just themselves. This requires open communication, active listening, and a willingness to compromise and work toward a common goal. By applying principles of Game Theory in this way, a team can work together to achieve success and avoid negative outcomes that can arise from a focus solely on self-interest.

In conclusion, I hope you can see the practical purposes that you can benefit from when making business decisions. Just as with any other strategy, you should never rely on a single method for every solution. It's important to understand the practical usage for the so it can be applied to benefit the situation in which it will prove beneficial. These are just strategies to help make better decisions, they don't actually make the decisions, but rather help guide you to a well informed decision.

Additional Thoughts

The probability distribution-based science of strategies discussed is referred to as a Game Theory. It models the logical and mathematical actions that members should take in order to achieve the best possible outcomes in the situations. Game Theory can look at everything from chess to tennis and everything from raising children to taking over a newly acquired company. However, there is one thing that all of these scenarios (games) share: their outcomes are dependent on each other's strategies.

Moreover, Game Theory is concerned with mathematical models of conflicts and cooperation among rational decision-makers. The study of decision-making in games in which players must devise strategies that affect the interests of other players are why the constructs of Game Theory exist.

Any scenario with two or more players with known payoffs, or quantifiable outcomes, is thought to be compatible with Game Theory. Players can use this theory to figure out the most likely outcomes while also considering the choices and actions of others that will affect the outcome.

According to game theory, players in a game will strive to maximize their advantages/rewards in order to win. Game theory has many applications outside of economics, such as in psychology, warfare, politics, and notably business.

Make sure to use the skills responsibly because being reckless with this principle can be detrimental. Be responsible, not just for your sake, but also for others' sake.

Much as with all situational theories, it is best to know your audience. Knowing your audience is a key component in gaining control of the situation, and as a leader being able to control the situation is highly significant.

Chapter 6

Strategizing with Psychology

Every successful company should have a strategic vision and where it should lead them in pursuit of the goal(s). Before a business or a team expects to be successful at achieving their goals they must know the value that planning and goal-setting play in the long-term. Without understanding where you want to end up, your measure of success is ambiguous and unreachable. To compound the problem, without a plan the achievable marks of success are not realizable.

Psychologists have looked at teamwork in the modern workplace and discovered that certain psychological traits could increase the likelihood of team success when developed, focused, and cultivated (or motivated). Understanding people's psychological needs and meeting those needs at work is extremely beneficial to leaders and the company overall. Benefits can range from increased employee satisfaction to increased overall productivity.

An essential skill in one's personal and professional life is leadership. While bad leadership can evoke disaster, good leadership can help ensure success. Understanding various psychological concepts can prove highly beneficial for effective leadership.

Great leaders are made, not born. Even though there is no one-size-fits-all formula for success (nor should there be, because it would limit creativity), there are psychological principles that can assist you in becoming a more effective leader. Here are seven of the most crucial psychological concept to master to become an effective leader:

1. The Principle of Authority

Providing instructions to others is not enough to be an effective leader. Because people are complex beings, you need to know how they think and what drives and motivates them, aiming to get the most out of them for the best outcome. A great leader has a deep knowledge of human psychology.

According to the Authority Principle, people are more likely to follow those in positions of authority (e.g., "the boss," law enforcement, professors, and doctors). By making sure your subordinates understand the boundaries of your authority as a leader, you can use this principle to your advantage. Often, when your authority is unquestioned and you have established trust, your orders will be carried out with your vision in mind.

Use this principle with great care. People will quickly lose respect for you if you abuse your position of authority. Instead, utilize your authority to motivate and influence others and assist them in achieving their objectives in service of company goals.

Your staff needs to know you are in charge and have the capability, experience, and expertise necessary to make decisions in favor of the business and the team. When communicating with your team, being concise and clear is the best way to demonstrate authority. Be available to answer any questions they may have and ensure that your instructions are easily comprehendible (*clear, concise, and understandable*). By being decisive and consistent in your decision-making, you can show your team your confidence in your abilities. People will be more likely to respect your opinion and listen to what you have to say if they see you are self-assured and able to establish and maintain order.

2. The Principle of Social Proof

According to this principle, people are expected to do something when they observe other people doing it. Peer pressure can be so persuasive because of this (although this is a negative application). So, how can an effective leader make better use of social proof in leadership?

To become a person that others truly admire and look up to in the workplace, you must be someone that colleagues genuinely want to follow. By showing dedication, pushing boundaries, and exhibiting healthy leadership, you can inspire others to do the same. Much of it is built on trust. You can also encourage members of your team to give each other constructive criticism (in a safe and engaging manner). Team members will be more likely to reciprocate when they see that their coworkers value and respect them.

You can develop an atmosphere where people feel at ease discussing their accomplishments and sharing their insights and knowledge. Team members will be more likely to contribute and grow if they see their colleagues are encouraged to do so. Your ability to influence those around you is a crucial leadership skill.

3. The Principle of Reciprocity

According to the principle of reciprocity, we are more likely to help someone who has previously helped us. This occurs daily, from small acts of kindness to important business deals.

Reciprocity can be used to enhance leadership. For instance, if you want your team to be more helpful to one another, you should model what it looks like to be helpful. Offer to assist someone having trouble with a task. Go out of your way to help, do so organically without keeping score (otherwise, reciprocity will backfire and feel like a chore or an obligation), and make it a regular practice.

Not only will you make their work simpler, you will make it more likely they will assist you in return.

Reciprocity helps foster a sense of teamwork and cooperation and increases employee productivity and engagement. Why? Because they're part of a supportive team.

4. The Principle of Likability

Wouldn't you rather follow a leader who you respect and admire? When a leader is likable, they will be much easier to follow. Fortunately, you can make yourself more likable as a leader.

First and foremost, be authentic in your interactions with others. Since insincerity is easily discernible, being genuine is essential for winning people over, and it has to come from the heart (this can be learned by focusing on empathy). Second, show that you care about those you're leading. Inquire about their lives, families, interests, and more – take a personal interest. People need to know that you care about them and that they matter to you. Third, simply be positive. This may take a great deal of intentionality and effort (especially some days). Nobody wants to be surrounded by negativity. You should also be modest and humble. A boastful leader who believes they are superior to others is typically disliked. Finally, showing appreciation for someone's accomplishments can significantly increase their admiration and respect for you as a leader.

5. The Principle of Scarcity

People are more likely to value tangible and intangible products, ideas, and resources if they are scarce, and this holds true for social resources also. A limited-edition item, for instance, is more likely to be appreciated or valued by consumers over something mass-produced. The same can be said for resources like time and attention.

People will feel valued and appreciated if you give them your full attention when spending time with them. Similarly, giving people your time will make them feel valued and important.

With this principle, you can protect your time and intentionally make it harder for people to reach you instantaneously. When you share your time with others, they will appreciate it more. By reducing the frequency of interactions, the value of your time increases.

When you are asked to give of your time or energy, it's okay to say "no". When allowing yourself to say "no", you create scarcity around your time and energy. Consequently, people will realize they must carefully prioritize what they ask of you. By applying the scarcity principle, you can increase your value as a leader and foster deeper relationships with the people you work with.

6. The Principle of Consistency

Leaders who are consistent in their words, deeds, and actions tend to attract followers. If you want people who respect and trust you as a leader, you must communicate clearly and consistently.

People will quickly lose confidence in you as a leader if you say one thing but do another or if you constantly change your mind. People are more likely to trust and respect you if they know what to expect from you. Credibility and expertise are both enhanced by consistency and stability.

People are more inclined to view you as a leader who *deserves* to be followed if you are known for keeping your promises. Consistency applies to your behavior as well. Your team will quickly lose trust in your leadership abilities if you consistently miss meetings or deadlines. On the other hand, they will be more interested to follow your lead if you are consistently on time and focused on meeting deadlines or the task at hand.

7. The Principle of Reinforcement

If you want your team to triumph, you must celebrate and encourage them. There are numerous ways to do this, such as providing feedback, offering incentives, and establishing clear expectations. You can use reinforcement as a leader to get your team members to effectively behave in a certain way.

You can offer encouragement and rewards for coming up with new ideas if you want your team to be more creative. Incentivize areas you want improvement on in order to generate buy-in. Not only will it make it more likely that those actions will be repeated, but it will also improve morale and motivation.

It is essential to refrain from reprimanding or punishing people publicly. Punishment can be used to restructure behavior but should be done so in private. Punishment should be centered around a plan to actively improve performance. There is a time and place for discipline to correct behavior, but it should be done through open communication and give the individual an opportunity to improve constructively. Unconstructive punishment (especially when done publicly) will likely reduce creativity and productivity and have no beneficial outcome. As a leader, positive reinforcement should be your primary focus to achieve your desired objective. Using positive reinforcement, you can create an environment where your team feels supported and motivated to reach their full potential. In turn, this creates a workplace where team members flourish.

Additional Thoughts

Understanding and meeting the psychological needs of team members contribute to increased employee satisfaction and overall productivity. Developing and cultivating teamwork-focused psychological traits enhances team success.

Leadership plays a crucial role in personal and professional life. Great leaders are made, not born, and understanding psychological concepts can help improve leadership effectiveness.

The Seven Crucial Psychological Concepts for Effective Leadership we discussed are summarized below:

Principle of Authority: Utilize authority to motivate and influence others while maintaining trust and boundaries.

Principle of Social Proof: Inspire others by being someone they admire and follow, encouraging trust and constructive criticism within the team.

Principle of Reciprocity: Model helpfulness to foster teamwork and cooperation, increasing employee productivity and engagement.

Principle of Likability: Be authentic, caring, positive, humble, and appreciative to become a likable leader.

Principle of Scarcity: Value and appreciate time and attention, protect your time, and say "no" when necessary to increase your value as a leader.

Principle of Consistency: Communicate clearly and consistently, keep promises, and be reliable to gain trust and respect as a leader.

Principle of Reinforcement: Celebrate and encourage team members through feedback, incentives, and clear expectations, using positive reinforcement to create a supportive and motivated work environment.

By understanding these psychological concepts, leaders can become more effective in motivating their teams, fostering cooperation, and reaching the intended goals.

CHAPTER 7

Soft Skills in the Team

When operating as a team in well-defined alignment, then collaboration and communication—essential components of well-structured teamwork—flow intuitively and are more likely to become habits.

So, how does one form an effective team? The Team Emotional and Social Intelligence (TESI) Model identifies seven necessary competencies.

1. Team Identity

When a group's identity is aligned with individual team members' strengths and personality traits, it supports a sense of belonging, a willingness to cooperate, and a feeling of clarity around every part of the job. Loyalty is high among groups that share a strong sense of team identity.

2. Motivation

A high level of motivation correlates with team energy and responsibility, as well as the degree to which competition is working in the team's favor or against it. Knowing and pursuing a desire, setting stretch goals, emphasizing success, and persevering are all necessary for a team to be motivated (and can even create a willingness to push further).

3. Emotional Intelligence and Awareness

The degree to which a team pays attention to, comprehends, and respects the feelings of its members is referred to as its emotional intelligence. Emotional intelligence plays a crucial role in a team's emotional awareness, encompassing the degree to which team members pay attention to, comprehend, and respect each other's feelings. By cultivating emotional intelligence within the team, individuals become more attuned to the emotions of their colleagues, which fosters a supportive and empathetic environment. This heightened emotional awareness positively impacts motivation, productivity, and the team's ability to collaborate effectively. It empowers team members to understand and address any underlying emotions that influence their behaviors and decisions, leading to stronger relationships, enhanced communication, and the success of the team as a whole.

4. Communication

Healthy communication in group collaboration is reflective of how well each team member listens, encourages participation, and allows for the discussion of sensitive subjects.

5. Stress Tolerance

A team with a high-stress tolerance is aware of how well it manages the pressures of a busy schedule, limited time, and the need for work-life balance. A team that can tolerate stress can take on highly impactful work and is not limited by internal or external stressors.

6. Conflict Resolution

To assess a team's conflict resolution abilities, one must look at how the team handles disagreements and whether it can use adversity to improve performance rather than allowing it to take over. Find an open and objective way to help the team feel safe to express problems that arise. With proper direction and guidance toward healthy conflict resolution, a team can grow and prosper in astounding ways.

7. Positive Mood

Encouragement, a bit of humor, and an expectation of success are foundational for building a team with a positive attitude. Positive temperament is a central point in a group's adaptability and strength. It's the core of a "can-do" mentality and impacts the team's enthusiasm.

When you are intentional about having a positive temperament, the team will be productive, and their emotional and social well-being will be improved. According to Henry Ford, "Coming together is the beginning. Keeping together is progress. Working together is success."

Time Management

Many of us attempt to solve time management issues through processes. To-do lists are written, tasks are scheduled in our calendars, and time management apps are downloaded. However, none of these is the answer. Time management is rooted in our actions. Disciplined, dedicated, and diligent intentionality goes into creating processes that work. A great deal of energy needs to be spent on simplifying work. **In a world surrounded by complexity, strive for simplicity.**

Leadership consultants Robert H. Schaffer and Ron Ashkenas surveyed over 1,300 managers and found that only 47% of their work time was spent on managerial tasks. Instead of leading, the remaining time was spent on more familiar, hands-on tasks (Tank 2023).

We naturally gravitate toward activities that give us a false sense of control because we believe that by helping employees with their work, we give our teams permission to delegate to us or fill their perceived need for an immediate solution without fully considering the long-term effects.

Here are some tips around productivity and prioritization that will help your team and your skills as a leader.

Embrace the intersection

Psychologist Jordan Peterson explained that life is "intense, gripping, and meaningful" at the intersection of chaos and order.

Total order would prevent us from exploring the unknown and learning new things, while total chaos would be overwhelming. In many ways, our work operates under the same constraints. To stay productive, consistency and well-defined planning are essential. And we need to explore and innovate to take our business and education to the next level. We must welcome uncertainty but not allow it to cause chaos. As simple as this sounds, this is actually the nexus of where a good leader becomes so important. A leader grounded in the ability to see future needs while balancing those with opportunities for innovation takes a great deal of discipline and is very rare. That lack of certainty is a challenging place of discomfort for many. However, when uncertainty is harnessed and embraced, it can be rewarding – not only for the leader but also for the team and the company.

FOCUS AND ENTHUSIASM

Enthusiasm, when consciously focused on a specific task, (or an energetic enthusiasm) is a driver that inspires us to tackle challenging projects and overwhelming workloads.

Focus involves zeroing in on a goal and seeing it through to completion. This includes putting off responding to every email and scheduling meetings that can wait. Accepting risk and uncertainty can deplete a leader's focus and energy.

Research Behind Accepting Risk and Uncertainty

According to a recent study, our brain dislikes uncertainty more than a negative outcome. Our limbic system produces a strong threat response when we perceive uncertainty in the future. This causes us to experience anxiety, which makes it harder for us to concentrate. Our brain thinks something might be wrong and relays a response to the body for more energy, in a real sense emptying us of the energy we need to complete our tasks for the day.

Chronic tension and stress (due to the anxiousness caused by uncertainty) can cause a sleeping disorder, creating a repeating pattern of decline in one's physical and mental health. The lack of sleep harms our working memory and drains our energy. It's a never-ending perpetuating cycle. Some certain level of uncertainty is necessary for our everyday decision-making. Still, as a good leader, mitigating risk in this area is vital to minimize uncertainty where possible.

The process seems to result in a paradoxical intention residing in the fact that *what is needed* and *what is done* may be at odds with each other due to the pressure of disrupting thought patterns. If you notice one of your direct reports experiencing anxiety, suggesting they "calm down" may cause more anxiety. Most people have not been trained to regulate their internal self-talk or the physiological state of their mental processes. At a minimum, having awareness of the anxiety and what's causing can be invaluable in helping alleviate symptoms.

However, not all anxiety due to stress or uncertainty is a bad thing. Our bodies and brains experience eustress, a positive kind of stress when we know we can cope with a difficult task in front of us; eustress provides us with energy and motivation and helps push us forward.

Our heart and breathing rates increase as a result of anxiety, which also causes the release of hormones meant to keep us alert and awake. If you're trying to solve a problem and meet a tight deadline, this can be helpful for a limited amount of time.

Shifting from anxiousness to excitement can be a more effective way to manage our emotions, as it helps us feel more energized and perform better. Instead of trying to calm ourselves down, which may result in a perpetual state of reinforced anxiety, we can reframe our thoughts and embrace what we're feeling as excitement or an opportunity. By deliberately shifting our focus to the potential positive aspects of the situation, we can fuel our enthusiasm and significantly improve our performance. This approach, called "cognitive reframing," is simpler and more rationally plausible than attempting to alter our physiological response to anxiety. Rather than trying to diminish our fear, we can redirect our attention and reshape our perception to make it a source of motivation and drive.

More on Thought Management

If you are nervous about changing your work schedule, try reframing it by telling yourself, "I hope something new and unexpected comes up today." If you're dreading the possibility of a subordinate not accomplishing a task, try reframing that dread as, "Whether or not, my employee completes the task on time, I am going to learn something valuable." Restructure the challenge into an opportunity.

Another method to help manage thoughts and fears is paradoxical intention. You're intentionally facing your fears to overcome them. Let's say you're afraid of being unable to improve your performance. You would say to yourself, "I hope I struggle to improve and make a mistake because once I solve those challenges, I'll be better for it." Paradoxical intention may appear illogical, but neurologists have been able to successfully use it for decades to assist individuals in overcoming their greatest fears.

In some ways, thought management can be more important to productivity than time management.

Digging deeper: Case study research

Naomi Eisenberger, a leading researcher in social neuroscience at the (UCLA) University of California, Los Angeles, wanted to know how people's brains work when they feel rejected by others. She devised an experiment in which volunteers participated in a cyberball-themed computer game while having their brains scanned by a Functional Magnetic Resonance Imaging (fMRI) machine. Cyberball is reminiscent of the game played at the school playground. Eisenberger explains, "People thought they were playing a game of ball tossing over the internet with two other people." They were able to see avatars for two additional people in addition to their own self-representative avatar. The subjects stopped receiving the ball about halfway through the game of catch between the three of them, and the two other alleged players threw the ball only to each other. The game players reported experiencing feelings of resentment, rejection, or judgment even after learning that no other human players were involved as if the other avatars excluded them for some reason.

The brain's responses could be directly connected to this reaction. "Activity was observed in the dorsal region of the anterior cingulate cortex, which is the neural region responsible for the distressing or suffering aspects of pain. — when people felt excluded," says Eisenberger. In this area, the most active people were those who felt rejected the most. To put it another way, the experience of being excluded elicited the same kind of response in the brain as physical pain might.

We as humans constantly evaluate the ways in which social interactions either raise or lower our status. Hidehiko Takahashi's research that was published in 2009, shows that when individuals understand that they could contrast horribly with another person, the dangerous reaction kicks in, delivering cortisol and other pressure-related chemicals. (The biological marker of the threat response that is accurate is cortisol. Cortisol levels rise in response to low self-esteem, which is linked to chronic anxiety and sleep deprivation.)

You can change your schedule and put things off until later whenever you want. However, neither a system nor an application can assist you in breaking free from the never-ending cycle of inefficiency and ineffectiveness.

Leaders can assist with simplify thought management with their employees by doing away with outdated organizational practices that inevitably cause undue stress. For instance, performance evaluations frequently elicit a threat response. Because of this, 360-degree reviews may be ineffective at bringing about positive behavioral change unless they are extremely participative and well-designed. Similarly, simply asking, "Can I give you some advice?" tends to invoke an auto-defense response because there is a tendency to assume the person offering advice is claiming to be superior. Hearing footsteps in the dark is the cortisol equivalent of this experience. This shouldn't preclude you from giving feedback, but it helps raise awareness of more constructive methods to provide such feedback. Know your audience when offering feedback so it can be received constructively and its benefit can be maximized.

A promotion is often seen as the only way to elevate an employee's status within an organization. However, this couldn't be further from the truth. Perceptions of status also rise when an employee receives compliments or commendations. According to Keise Izuma's 2008 experiments, a computer simply saying "good job" affects the same reward mechanisms in the brain as a financial windfall. When someone learns a new skill, their sense of status also rises. Rather than based on their seniority, paying employees more for their skills boosts their status. Align people well with their strengths because they will feel a positive sense of purpose and value when they complete their work.

Status is strongly influenced by values. Organizations that attempt to pit individuals against one another in the hope that doing so will force them to work harder reinforce the notion that there are only winners and losers, which harms the status of those not among the company hierarchy or elite.

A person's brain goes into a kind of automatic pilot mode when they are in a routine situation to save energy: It is based on long-standing neural connections in the motor cortex and basal ganglia that have, in effect, hardwired the individual's response to this type of situation. This makes it simple for the individual to perform previous actions and frees them to perform two tasks simultaneously, for instance, to converse while driving. However, the brain triggers an error signal as soon as it detects ambiguity or confusion, such as when the car in front of the driver applies the brakes. The driver needs to stop talking as soon as the threat response kicks in and their working memory gets worse, and they need to pay full attention to the road.

In the part of the brain known as the anterior cingulate cortex, uncertainty is perceived as an error, gap, or tension: something that needs to be fixed before one can feel again at ease. People crave certainty for this reason. Due to the fact that it requires additional neural energy, not knowing what will happen next can be extremely debilitating. Memory declines, performance suffers, and people lose interest in the now.

Obviously, uncertainty is not always crippling. Interest and attention are drawn to mild uncertainty: People's adrenaline and dopamine levels rise just enough in response to new and challenging circumstances to pique their curiosity and motivate them to solve problems. In addition, people respond to uncertainty in the world in a variety of ways, some of which are influenced by pre-existing thought patterns. For instance, the driver who wonders, "What should I do?", when the car in front suddenly comes to a stop is probably ineffective, whereas the driver who makes the situation manageable by stating, "I need to move left now because there's a car on the right" is well-prepared to respond. Life itself can be uncertain. Focus and performance suffer when there is an overabundance of uncertainty perceived. People panic and make poor choices when their perception of uncertainty grows out of control.

A Leader Creates Certainty Where There is None

To build self-assured and committed well-performing teams, managers and leaders must work to create a perception of certainty. This perception is enhanced by transparency, sharing business plans, and providing precise organizational structure maps. People are more likely to trust a plan and feel a sense of certainty about it when it's transparent and explains how decisions are made.

The feeling of certainty can also be facilitated by breaking down complicated projects into manageable steps. Even though it is highly doubtful everything will go according to plan, the project now appears less ambiguous, which helps people function better. An employee focused on a single, manageable task is unlikely to have a limbic system in overdrive generating feelings of anxiety.

Psychological Maturity and Motivation

Psychological maturity is essential for effective leadership. According to the author Abraham Gitlow, a psychologically insecure leader will often lead in a "traditional, hierarchical, pyramidal, top-down way" (Gitlow 2004), with a focus on positional authority. In contrast, an emotionally stable and mature leader will often choose to lead in a more horizontal, diffused, and participative manner. Gitlow explained that followers might develop self-discipline when leadership and positional authority are combined. This results in voluntary self-introspection, which means the desire to perform at one's best comes from within rather than being imposed. In a nutshell, Gitlow argued that follower cooperation was doomed to fail under an insecure and immature leader.

Great Leaders Create Psychological Safety

Fostering a sense of belonging and embracing collaboration are both crucial to the success of a company. These elements play a pivotal role in creating a positive and thriving work environment, where individuals feel valued, included, and motivated to contribute their best. Further research shows that employee retention rates have decreased by 50%, and productivity has increased by 56% in organizations that create a strong sense of belonging.

What does that imply?

Amy Edmondson, a professor at Harvard Business School, came up with the term "psychological safety," which she defines as, "A shared belief that the team is safe for interpersonal risk-taking." In an environment with a high level of psychological safety, people are permitted to speak up and express their thoughts. Psychological safety is just as important to an effective team as performance standards and physical safety.

Psychological safety entails feeling secure and confident in expressing one's thoughts, ideas, and opinions without fear of judgment, ridicule, or shame. It serves as a critical foundation for establishing trust and breaking down barriers in both professional and personal relationships. Without fostering psychological safety, it becomes challenging to build strong and cohesive teams and hinders collaboration, growth, and development of a thriving organizational culture. In Maslow's Hierarchy of Needs, safety is an essential basic human need. To drive the point further, establishing a mentally safe workplace is a basic necessity for high-performing groups. This promotes employee retention and the ability to collaborate and communicate openly.

There are numerous advantages to creating a psychologically safe work environment including:

Enhanced employee engagement: It's easier for team members to get involved when they feel safe at work. This could happen in a team meeting, when they solve problems, work together on projects, and interact with customers and colleagues.

Fosters a diverse workplace culture: Including diverse people and perspectives on the team is more important than ever. Diverse teams help propel creativity and thrive better in secure workplaces. The end result is a rich experience of giving and receiving in which everyone feels connected and part of a cohesive unit.

Encourages creativity and new ideas: Team members must feel comfortable expressing themselves so ideas and creativity flow naturally and organically. Imagine how many brilliant concepts remained unshared because a team member did not feel psychologically safe.

Improved employee well-being: Mental health is the state of one's psychological and emotional well-being; it can include mental illness, but, by definition, is not synonymous with mental illness or deficiency. Mental health has a significant impact on overall well-being. Employees perform better and avoid or manage stressors that prevent them from doing their best when they are mentally healthy.

It creates brand ambassadors: When team members are treated fairly, they cannot help but share about how wonderful their work is.

Reduced employee turnover: According to a recent study, team members are less likely to leave their jobs if they feel psychologically safe. Why ditch a company that treats you with respect and offers a sense of security and worth?

Besides, interviewing, hiring, and training all come with tremendous expense. A business that doesn't bake psychological safety into its culture will likely have high employee turnover, which is unsustainable.

Boosts team performance: Teams perform when they have employees who are highly engaged and unwilling to leave. Teams perform when there are brand ambassadors, inspired ideas, and inclusive workplace culture.

According to the adage, *actions speak louder than words*. Leaders' actions and reactions are reflected in team culture. Organizational harm can result from leaders who fail to create and support psychologically safe team environments.

Putting it All Together

To build a high-performing team, you must cultivate a strong sense of trust, which is achievable if the team feels psychologically safe.

The first step in creating a psychologically safe workplace is leader alignment and coaching that focuses on behavioral change. This begins with every team and member and extends throughout the organization. To change cultural norms, everyone in the company must learn together over time. An individual coach who oversees these processes ensures that behavior changes are taught correctly. Experiential learning reinforces it in real time. Leaders must consistently model the intended behaviors in order to establish new team norms and maintain a psychologically safe work environment.

Additional Thoughts

Positive psychological and cognitive research assists pioneers with seeing and fostering the qualities in their workers as opposed to mischaracterizing them as shortcomings. Positive psychology can be used by leaders to instill in their staff members a "growth mindset," which emphasizes effort, receiving feedback in a collaborative and ongoing manner, and informal collaboration for improvement. Working toward a common goal at work can assist leaders in developing and directing each employee's growth process.

Relationships are the most important aspect of leadership. Concepts from positive psychology encourage employees and managers to communicate frequently, which helps team members feel valued. Positive and constructive communication on a consistent basis is one of the single most powerful tool for fostering an environment that is productive, secure, and friendly.

Psychological safety creates an environment where individuals can freely express themselves, leading to increased innovation and productivity.

Chapter 8

Components of Effective Social Intelligence in Leadership

Imagine a leader who effortlessly commands respect, inspires unwavering loyalty, and consistently drives exceptional results. What sets these extraordinary leaders apart from the rest? It goes beyond mere charisma or technical expertise—exceptional leaders have a unique talent for understanding and connecting with others, which are two of several integral components of social intelligence.

Strength of character, empathy, mindfulness, consciousness, emotional intelligence, and the relentless pursuit of learning help contribute to an impactful and emotionally intelligent leader. Each is pivotally important in building authentic connections, fostering a positive work environment, and unleashing the full potential of your team.

Let's dive deeper into these concepts so we can lean into your true potential as a leader and take your skills to the next level. Here are some essential components of a socially intelligent leader:

STRENGTH OF CHARACTER

As author Robert Dilenschneider emphasizes, a leader must have strong character to rally a great following and gain trust. Strength of character involves demonstrating integrity, honesty, and a commitment to ethical behavior. A leader who lacks these qualities is unlikely to earn the trust and loyalty of their followers. To maintain trust, leaders must remain consistent in their behavior and decision-making, even in challenging situations. Demonstrating strength of character helps leaders inspire and motivate their teams, even in the face of adversity, leading to greater success and achievement.

EMPATHY

Empathy involves reasoning, understanding, and relating to others on a deep level. When leaders possess empathy, they can genuinely connect with their team members' unique perspectives and emotions. By actively listening and demonstrating empathy, leaders create an environment where individuals feel heard, valued, and understood.

Being both compassionate and focused is essential for leaders to navigate the complexities of leading a team. Leaders must actively and authentically listen to others, considering the needs of the individual while balancing them with the needs of the team and company.

Empathy is a uniquely powerful tool for making others feel heard and acknowledged. By practicing empathy, leaders show genuine care and interest in the experiences and emotions of their team members. Empathy creates a sense of connection and shared understanding, fostering trust and collaboration within the team.

When leaders combine empathy with a focus on goals and outcomes, they create a dynamic leadership style that blends the needs and well-being of individuals while still driving toward success. Integration of empathy and focus enhances leadership effectiveness and promotes a positive work environment where team members feel supported and motivated.

Emotional Intelligence (*or* EQ)

The term "emotional intelligence" was used first by Daniel Goleman and refers to a person's capacity to read and interpret the feelings and perspectives of others. When a leader shows emotional intelligence, it creates an environment where employees feel at ease and lower their defenses. This relaxed state promotes open communication and trust. By empathizing with their followers, leaders establish a strong connection and foster an atmosphere of understanding and support.

In a survey conducted by CareerBuilder in collaboration with TalentSmart (an EQ provider), it was found that 71 percent of employers prioritize emotional intelligence (EQ) over intellectual intelligence (IQ). According to the survey, these employers believe that individuals with strong emotional intelligence are better equipped to remain composed during challenging situations, adeptly resolve conflicts, and demonstrate empathy towards their colleagues. (Landry 2019).

Four core competencies of emotional intelligence include:

1. Self-awareness

2. Self-management

3. Social awareness

4. Relationship management

Self-Awareness

Self-awareness is your capacity to recognize your strengths and weaknesses as well as your emotions and their impact on your performance and that of your team.

Tasha Eurich, an organizational psychologist, conducted research that found 95% of people believe they are self-aware, but only 10% to 15% actually are. This can cause issues for your employees. Eurich's research shows that working with coworkers who aren't self-aware can reduce a team's success by half and cause more stress and less motivation.

Leaders need to maintain the ability to be self-aware because you must first bring out the best in yourself before you can bring out the best in others. By completing 360-degree feedback, in which your performance is assessed, and then comparing it to the assessments of your chief, peers, and direct reports, you can easily evaluate your self-awareness. Through this process, you will learn more about your own behavior and how the organization sees you.

Self-Management

Self-management is the ability to control your emotions, especially in stressful situations, and keep a positive outlook despite setbacks. Leaders who can't self-manage are more likely to react and have a harder time with impulse control.

Reactions are usually instinctive. However, the more in tune you are with your emotional intelligence, the simpler it will be to think, breathe, and take a step back before reacting.

Social Awareness

Understanding and managing one's own emotions is essential, but so is knowing how to read a room. Your capacity for social awareness is your capacity to recognize the dynamics at play within your organization as well as the emotions of others.

Leaders who excel in social awareness also practice empathy. These leaders strive to understand the correlation between perspectives and feelings of their coworkers, which enables them to communicate and collaborate more effectively.

According to DDI, a global company that specializes in leadership development, mastering empathy is the most important leadership skill because it increases a leader's performance in areas such as coaching, engaging others, and making decisions by more than 40%. According to Middle for Innovative Administration, managers who exhibit greater empathy for their subordinates are rated higher by superiors (Landry 2019).

You can support your team better and boost your own performance at the same time if you communicate with empathy.

Relationship Management

Relationship management involves influencing, coaching, mentoring, and successfully resolving conflicts.

According to research, gossip and other unproductive activities can consume approximately eight hours of company time for each unresolved conflict, draining resources and morale. While it's important to properly address issues as they arise, some prefer to avoid conflict. You need to have hard conversations if you want to keep your team happy. The Society for Human Resource Management's recent survey revealed "respectful treatment of all employees at all levels" was cited by 72% of workers as the most important aspect of job satisfaction (Landry 2019).

Nonverbal Communication...

Everyone expresses emotions and thoughts using nonverbal communication. Interpreting nonverbal body language can present unique challenges to understanding and communicating with others at work. You must be able to effectively communicate with coworkers, supervisors, and interviewers through gestures, tone of voice, and other nonverbal cues, regardless of whether you are working in person or remotely.

Through non-verbal communication, people can convey happiness, engagement, concern, gratitude, and confidence. Hand gestures, eye contact, body language, appearance, facial expressions, and tone of voice all fall under non-verbal communication.

Here are some examples to help you become more adept at nonverbal communication in the workplace:

Proper Eye Contact

If coworkers know they are heard, they will feel valued and appreciated. Make eye contact with them as they speak to help them feel this way. They will know you are listening attentively to what they have to say if you focus on them rather than your computer, paperwork, or mobile phone. Turning on your camera for video chats can build a respectful relationship between coworkers, and keeping eye contact while responding to them also keeps the conversation interesting.

Example: A colleague approaches you with an idea to improve departmental collaboration. By maintaining eye contact and nodding in agreement, you can demonstrate you are paying attention.

THE POSITIVE TONE OF VOICE

Always be aware of your tone of voice so you convey your intended message. Keeping a positive tone when talking with a coworker or supervisor can affect the energy of the entire conversation.

Example: An employee is presenting a new client engagement strategy. To get people excited about the project, the employee speaks with vigor and positivity. As a result of the employee's enthusiasm, senior management's interest in the project rises.

PERSONAL APPEARANCE

The way you present yourself can have a bigger impact than the words you speak. Even if you're in the comfort of your home office, maintaining a tidy workstation or looking neat and prepared can convey confidence and make a good impression on coworkers.

Example: You hope to speak with a supervisor to ask for a raise or promotion. Dress professionally to demonstrate your dedication to the position and professionalism at work.

GOOD POSTURE

Whether you're standing or sitting, your posture can indicate how you feel about a situation or how attentive you are to a conversation. Sitting or standing straight can convey confidence.

Example: You want to communicate effectively because you have to present a new idea to your supervisor. Stand or sit with your shoulders back to show confidence and explain why you think the company will benefit from your idea.

FACIAL EXPRESSIONS

People frequently anticipate your nonverbal response by observing your facial expressions when you communicate with them. Keep in mind that even in a virtual interview, your face can convey your emotions and thoughts without words. When having a conversation, a smile, a nod, or the use of your eyebrows can convey a positive reaction.

Example: Smile and nod along with a coworker as they tell you about their recent vacation to show you enjoy their story.

PERSONAL SPACE

You may move closer to the person you are talking to during one-on-one conversations. This demonstrates that you want to hear them clearly and are interested in having a conversation. Try to give yourself enough room so that you and your partner can both feel at ease. However, if working with an employee originally from another country, learn about their culture first or ask them about personal space because it differs depending on one's region or culture of origin.

Example: Choose a closer seat to a coworker so you can hear them better before you sit down for a meeting.

Hand Gestures

Gestures and hand positions can convey feelings during conversations. People may become more focused on what you have to say if you use your hands to create expression during your stories. Additionally, hand gestures can convey friendliness or appreciation.

Example: A coworker is delivering a presentation, but they need to figure out how others will absorb it. They can see things are going well if you give them a casual but discrete "thumbs up".

Body Language

During a meeting or a conversation, body language can convey emotions. Crossing your arms may suggest you are closed off, whereas keeping your arms relaxed at your sides demonstrates openness and a willingness to listen. By leaning forward in your seat, you show politeness and that you're not paying attention to anything else.

Example: Sit straight with your arms on the table and watch a coworker present. This demonstrates your involvement in their presentation. They may conclude you are uninterested if you slouch in your seat.

Final Thoughts on Nonverbal Communication

You can gain a shared understanding of your coworkers' feelings, emotions, and attitudes by accurately interpreting their nonverbal cues. Collaboration with team members can boost productivity, engagement, and cultural competence if you can communicate with shared meaning.

Knowing how to communicate can also help you express your feelings about a variety of topics or situations. It can assist you with radiating confidence while conversing with bosses or expressing sympathy while paying attention to a colleague.

SITUATIONAL LEADERSHIP...

While emotional intelligence and understanding non-verbal communication help equip leaders to understand and connect with their team members on an individual level, Situational Leadership takes into account the dynamic nature of situations and the diverse needs of team members.

By seamlessly blending emotional intelligence Situational Leadership strategies, leaders can navigate the complexities of various scenarios and inspire optimal performance from their teams.

Situational Leadership places a strong emphasis on understanding your audience or employees. By leveraging psychological insights, leaders can strategically navigate different situations and adapt their approach to achieve positive results.

This method of leadership offers practicality and repeatability. The true essence of Situational Leadership lies in its application in various business settings. Leaders in organizations effectively utilize this model through different approaches, including:

Analyzing: Situational Leaders adjust their leadership style by focusing on the performance readiness of their team members. This enables them to adapt their approach based on the specific needs of each individual.

Adapting: These leaders are able to seamlessly adapt to the needs of multiple people in a room. They can quickly abandon the four influencing behaviors and tailor their approach to the unique circumstances at hand.

Influencing: Situational managers prioritize the cultivation of influence rather than relying solely on authority. They establish trust and create a secure work environment that encourages open communication and collaboration.

Serving: Situational Leadership is about helping others by being receptive to what employees want and need from their leader. By providing support and guidance, leaders foster an environment of growth and development.

Developing: A key goal of situational leaders is to help their followers develop. They act as mentors and colleagues, providing opportunities for growth and opening doors to valuable experiences.

By incorporating the principles of Situational Leadership, leaders can enhance their ability to influence others and create a positive impact within their organizations.

You can utilize any and all of these strategies to your advantage in your leadership role. Each opens up a unique opportunity to shift the outcome in your favor if used wisely.

Additional Thoughts

You will be able to empathize with others and communicate effectively if you comprehend where people are coming from and the reasons behind their actions. Understanding human behavior is the initial step in learning how to be a better boss.

You will have the tools you need to lead people more effectively once you have a solid understanding of these psychology's concepts. By really understanding your team's needs and meeting them, you'll be able to cut down on employee turnover and increase productivity. You will be able to develop each team member on an individual basis, fostering a sense of satisfaction, empowerment, and value from them. Finally, you'll be able to cultivate a sense of teamwork and loyalty among the team members that will ultimately result in business expansion and success.

Emotional intelligence allows leaders to understand and connect with their team members on a deeper level, fostering trust and collaboration. Nonverbal communication serves as a powerful tool for conveying messages and building rapport. And to tie all of the concepts together into an implementable process, situational leadership models helps to empower leaders to adapt their approach and navigate various situations for optimal results.

Chapter 9

Lean Startup & Agile Management

"Starting a company is like jumping off a cliff and assembling the plane on the way down." -Reid Hoffman

Leaders, innovators, and entrepreneurs worldwide utilize Lean startup techniques to transform brilliant ideas into outstanding products or services. In this chapter, we will discuss the benefits of Lean practices and what they can do for your organization.

In 2008, entrepreneur and author Eric Ries introduced the term "Lean Startup." After failing in his early entrepreneurship ventures, Eric Ries studied Lean manufacturing and implemented its principles in the startup industry.

Lean startup techniques apply to leadership even if you're not running a startup, viewing failure as an opportunity to promote growth. In many ways, it is a waste of time to construct five-year business plans around unknowns, and customer (or, in our case, team member) response is of the utmost importance.

Rather than strategies, Lean concepts revolve around a plan of action that can be attempted and proven or disproven quickly. It is not necessary to collect and analyze all the data before moving forward; it only needs to be adequate. At the point when clients don't respond as wanted, the startup rapidly acclimates to restrict its incorrect paths and returns to creating items that clients need.

On average, most people come up with an idea, write a business plan, and pitch it to various investors. Or they bootstrap it, launch the product, and begin selling it as hard as they can.

Translating Lean Startup to Leadership

Those who follow the traditional procedure laid out in the previous paragraph mistakenly believe the finest way to meet a goal is to build the solution, product, or process as soon as the idea hits, assuming once it's launched, customers will line up to buy, utilize, and consume it.

That fallacy is far from the truth. Most initial assumptions rarely hold true. But...what if you could guarantee the success of all your ideas in advance? With the Lean startup approach, it is certainly *possible*.

Lean focuses only on critically important tasks that create value and eliminates all wasteful processes—identifying early and often and adjusting where necessary. This means a startup's product life cycles will be shorter and that less time, money, and resources will be wasted. By employing this strategy, innovators can learn earlier whether their idea is successful and which strategy to pursue. Similarly, leaders seeking innovation can test and validate (refining processes, navigating efficiency and effectiveness, etc.) and pivot quickly when necessary.

Lean startup is broken down into five principles which include:

INNOVATORS AND GAME-CHANGERS ARE EVERYWHERE

This means the Lean Startup approach can be used across concepts, industries, or businesses – and in a similar fashion toward leadership principles. Being able to recognize those individuals, and help bring their skills together to ensure peak performance and success towards goals is where leadership becomes such a pivotal intrigue. Being able to capitalize on success of goals combined with utilizing someone's skills in conjunction with others that complement their skills in an orchestrated symphonic array of consistency is where "leadership" gets its meaning.

INNOVATION IS MANAGEMENT

Most people don't like management because they're more excited about *ideas* and *products*. However, they don't realize the long-term non-immediate potential a great leader can bring to the mix. The right leader in the right place can enable and influence the right direction. Albeit, in many cases, just as with life, good patterns don't instantaneously occur – they are the result of repeated disciplined patterns that span across the entire company. But they start with one leader, which spans to another leader, and so on – in essence, leaders create opportunities for other leaders to flourish. However, this doesn't happen overnight. It's a process, and it takes a lot of diligence and discipline.

VALIDATED LEARNING

Businesses should constantly pursue testing the practicality of their thoughts and plans. Startups can thus validate their ideas by learning what works and what doesn't on a consistent basis. This cycle of continued introspection to learn and grow helps to propel success in the long term.

INNOVATION ACCOUNTING

To cope with uncertainty, entrepreneurs must be held accountable and outcomes controlled. Innovation accounting can be used to accomplish this and includes: determining priorities for tasks and objectives, setting milestones, and measuring progress. Financial statements are a common standard measure of progress in established businesses. However, since most startups operate without revenue or profits, these statements are of little use to them. Therefore, innovation accounting controls outcomes and holds everyone accountable using a distinct set of metrics such as Acquisition, User Experience, User Retention, Referrals, and Revenue.

Build, Measure, and Learn

This is a feedback loop in which business owners construct goods based on their concepts, evaluate results, gain knowledge, and repeat the process until perfection is achieved. Because reducing waste of time, money, and resources is at the heart of lean, this entire feedback loop operates quickly. As a leader, this concept enables your team to innovate. Using that paradigm, you can expand on the concepts surrounding imperative learning patterns for driving innovation.

The Difference Between "*Lean*" and "*Agile*"

Although the terms "Agile" and "Lean" are frequently used to describe a team or organization, each refers to distinct approaches that address distinct issues. You'll find it simpler to determine which approach is most relevant to your organization if you are aware of the differences.

The capacity to invent and adapt to change is Agile. It is a strategy for coping with and thriving in a volatile and uncertain environment. It comes down to thinking about how to comprehend what is happening in your current environment, identifying any uncertainty, and figuring out how to adjust to it. This is where the difference in leadership capabilities is highly apparent between leaders and managers. This core concept highlights a skillset that allows a compounded rate of return – adaptability.

Being Agile means being able to respond quickly to the needs and demands of customers and the market (or your team's needs so they can best serve the needs of the customers) and changing course when necessary. The goal of Agile methodologies is to minimize the risk of creating products that do not or no longer satisfy market or customer needs while maximizing the value delivered to the customer. The primary method of offering these solutions in a scalable way is with great teams.

Agile methods have sought to shorten delivery times (delivering early, delivering frequently) to ensure that smaller vertical pieces of the product reach the market, allowing customers to provide early feedback while ensuring that the final product meets their requirements.

The basic tenet of the Agile philosophy is to improve workers' abilities, make work easier, and complete work within a well-defined amount of time.

As leaders, our aims are quite similar; we want to ensure we are enabling improvement in each workers' abilities, as they contribute to the overall team, to perform, make work more enjoyable, and enable opportunities to plan well so the team can accomplish work toward goals for a favorable outcome so they can share in success together.

Leaders can take advantage of Agile patterns and practices through similar processes and methods. To demonstrate this further, here are some of the most important concepts that tie leadership to Agile methods:

Focus on quality improvement:

To encourage prompt feedback, iterative development combines frequent demonstrations with comprehensive reviews. Agile teams adhere to the iteration process and anticipate rapidly changing market conditions. They concentrate on delivering a high-quality product while resolving any existing issues and requirements that are not well-defined or fully thought-out.

Collaboration:

Modern project management is incomplete without collaboration. Routine alignment meetings, review meetings, and planning meetings are all methods by which Agile fosters teamwork at all levels. In addition to making use of individual strengths and ideas, Agile teams create a workplace that is both productive and collaborative.

Quick learning and release:

Startups often face challenges that lead to a lack of time to investigate, troubleshoot, and perform proofs-of-concept. As a result, they must prioritize results over investment. The Agile process is simple to understand and use and has a short learning curve. In a similar vein, the Agile methodology aids in their learning, adaptation, and rapid launch of a minimum viable product.

Transparency:

In Agile methodology, teams and explicit stakeholders alike must provide feedback.

Additionally, in an Agile-like collaborative approach, tasks can be altered or eliminated throughout the process. This enables teams to eliminate ineffective features and make use of lucrative ones. Teams become more transparent as a result of Agile's motivation to complete featured tasks.

Result-Oriented:

Each cycle of work is effectively tracked and recorded in Agile development. The team uses daily alignment meetings to remove obstacles and keep track of the work progress leading toward their identified goals. Additionally, Agile development is not solely dependent on the outcome. There is a chance that the final product will get better with each iteration.

Putting it All Together

I hope you can see the convergence in value Agile and Lean can also offer leaders. Every business wants to develop a sustainable business model and produce quickly, affordably, and with low risk. This is one of the most advantageous areas that can help drive a measure of success as a leader.

The adoption of Lean and Agile principles offers valuable practices and patterns that can greatly support leaders in effectively managing their teams. By embracing Lean thinking and Agile methodologies, leaders can foster a culture of continuous improvement, adaptability, and collaboration. These principles provide a solid foundation for empowering teams, optimizing processes, and achieving outstanding results. As leaders embrace the concepts of Lean and Agile, they position themselves and their teams for success in today's dynamic and rapidly changing business landscape.

ADDITIONAL THOUGHTS

Eric Ries introduced the term "Lean Startup" in his 2011 book "The Lean Startup," describing it as an "Agile approach for structuring business processes and continuously adapting strategies where necessary." (Ries 2011) All internal production processes and decisions that don't add value to the customer and end-product are the primary focus of the Lean Startup approach. The Lean Startup philosophy's primary objective is to provide value to customers and eliminating procedures that do not contribute to this value can ultimately save a significant amount of time, effort, and money.

The iterative process of creating, testing, reviewing, and adjusting to ensure that the end user receives the ideal solution is the foundation of the definition of Agile. To better understand what the receiver wants and how they envision their ideal result, this feedback and adaptation loop is essential.

The focus of Agile is on effective communication between team members and their respective tools and tasks. The ability to move and think quickly, easily, and flexibly is the definition of agility, which is where term "Agile" comes from. In order to constantly meet the requirements of the customer, an Agile working method emphasizes constant awareness of change. Within the framework of Agile product management, every procedure is set up in such a way that it always becomes possible to modify particular aspects without having to put in a lot of effort or time.

By adopting Lean and Agile principles, you can enhance your leadership capabilities. These practices enable effective teamwork, foster innovation, and promote continuous learning. Embracing agility equips you to navigate change with confidence, inspire your team, and drive meaningful outcomes. Become a leader who excels in complexity and achieves remarkable success.

Chapter 10

Are Leaders Born or Made?

For decades, psychologists, scientists, and organizations alike have asked the question: are leaders born or made? Within the next dozen pages or so, we will unravel just that—and the answer may surprise you.

Organizations benefit greatly when they train their leaders. Leadership training should begin upon hiring or promotion; there's no need to wait for someone with natural leadership abilities to miraculously arrive on your doorstep. Although there is an opportunity cost associated with the time and resources required for leadership training, it offers many advantages.

- *More control over aligning with the mission and vision of the business.*
- *Allows for unified direction, ensuring everyone is being offered a standardized training.*

Many believe that some people inherently possess leadership skills while others do not. Think about the best leaders you've worked with. Chances are there was an effortlessness about their behavior and attitude that felt natural. It is not difficult to find business articles and books that list the qualities of these natural leaders, such as charisma or decisiveness. But are those qualities truly organic? Or can one *learn* leadership?

Let's begin with something that most of us agree on: Leadership ability is necessary. In addition, there is no universal definition of what makes a good leader as there is with most skills. Leaders can lead in a variety of ways, just like chefs can specialize in particular cuisines or musicians can master particular genres. One might be driven by data while another person might have excellent instincts for forecasting and trends. Another leader may be inspirational and sympathetic. Consider the best leaders you've ever worked with once more. None were exactly the same, were they?

Let's return to the query we posed in the chapter title: Are leaders *born* or *made*? As with any skill, some people naturally *excel* at leading, but one's propensity to excel at a given skill doesn't mean they were inherently born with the talents necessary to be an excellent leader. They are more likely willing to invest the time and dedication required to continually improve on the required skills. But in many ways, just having the time in the seat is much different than having focused time in the seat with a highly refined emphasis in the right areas that will drive future success in the leadership position. Using your time wisely is important.

Let's not forget that leaders positioned in the right areas to refine their skills in the right direction are going to be more likely to succeed. This is why leaders who surround themselves with talented colleagues have proven success.

Additionally, every successful leader has a journey marked by significant milestones that contribute to the development and refinement of their skills. These transformative experiences create a productive environment for personal growth, fostering an environment conducive to continuous improvement and excellence.

Unfortunately, many organizations are unaware of this (or don't have the capacity or ability to train toward this). They want to keep these outstanding individual contributors around. They, therefore, encourage them. They give them higher titles and more responsibility, and if they continue to perform well, a position in management will eventually follow. These leaders suddenly find themselves accountable for more than just the tangible work product. They are now in charge of people (and, in our particular area of interest, teams of people).

Consider a newly promoted manager. They have a proven track record of success doing well with previously assigned tasks and in certain roles. But now they need a whole new set of skills they didn't have before. Consider a salesperson now responsible not only for closing their own deals but also for the performance of their entire team. Or someone who has spent years as a software engineer but now needs to gather consensus and lead engineers. This could be a difficult task if these individuals are not *naturally* gifted leaders.

In many ways, it could be argued they have been set up to fail if not provided the right training for the opportunity. A study (2019) showed that 57% of frontline managers reported that trial and error helped them develop their leadership abilities. Companies cannot afford for new managers to wing it and hope for the best, as poor management accounts for 50% of attrition. (Muse 2019) And for this specific reason, leadership plays such a vital role in the overall scope.

It is essential, especially for new managers and emerging leaders, not to assume that being a great *contributor* automatically translates into being a great *leader*. It is an investment to give them that promotion and responsibility in the company, and you must keep investing by providing them with real leadership training. Coaching solutions, internal mentors, leadership books, conferences, and other options should be considered. And on the other side, as the leader, you must be committed to continually learning, which is an exciting and intriguing opportunity.

Leaders are not solely born with innate capabilities but rather hold the potential to be trained and developed. You can put money into solutions that help both learned and natural leaders become better leaders. Identify solutions that take a methodical, individual approach without overpromising.

Leadership is a deeply personal experience. However, authentic leadership is what sets good leaders apart from lesser ones. They are not acting, rather, they are being who they are. Passionate leaders tend to appear to lead effortlessly. One of the contributing factors to this is their ability to want to continue growing. The love for continued improvement naturally drives that desire. Doing something you love offers an intense level of meaning toward pushing further into it and allows you to go further without someone having to push you into it. Solutions and methods that pair new leaders with coaches or internal mentors are especially useful because they can help your leaders find and perfect the styles that come naturally to them, even if leading is not all that natural. In this case, self-awareness is a crucial factor, and solutions that treat leaders as individuals perform better than those that do not.

The question to focus on should not be whether leaders are born or made. Instead, we want to understand how to enhance the most out of each organization's leaders. And we do that by investing time and money to help leaders build toward their fullest potential.

The following are five teachable leadership traits that leaders should concentrate on to improve their leadership abilities.

1. **Goal Focused**: *A Clear, Achievable Vision*

True leaders create and convey a vision that motivates and inspires their team. This necessitates a passion for the vision, the clarity to convey it, and the experience and intelligence to carry it out. Create a concise vision for yourself first, so you can guide your team to the intended goal. Whether you prefer to use a vision board or a list, start writing down some of your most important objectives and goals immediately. Be specific, but do not limit yourself. For instance, don't just say that you want to reach a certain distance; instead, set your goals higher and aim for more significant achievements. In the end, you want each goal to have a timetable and a measurable outcome.

Lay out some small steps or establish routines and habits to help you achieve your goal. You will be better equipped to inspire others to set and achieve their own goals the more you practice doing so.

2. **Trustworthy and Confident**: *The Ability to Inspire and Influence*

Keep in mind that your work and its success are not solely your responsibility. Good leaders know how to get the people around them to work together toward a common objective. Leverage this as an opportunity to practice this skill whenever you are pitching an idea, communicating an innovative way to proceed with a process, or introducing a big new project to your team. Take some time to carefully plan how you will facilitate an emotional connection between people and your idea while demonstrating to them that moving forward is entirely doable with the assistance of a few tactical steps. If great ideas are not conveyed effectively, they may be lost, so practice and perfect this! Practicing your pitch with a companion can be extraordinarily helpful for improvement.

3. **Adaptability: The Capacity to Adapt**

A good leader understands how to deal with change and shape change to be a positive experience for the team. Change should not be seen as a challenge but rather an opportunity to be creative, flexible, and decisive in the face of uncertainty. It is also a great time to demonstrate to others that you can trust them to make important decisions.

Getting over the panic that can set in during a shifting situation—or at least becoming more comfortable with it—is one of the initial steps in learning this skill because change can be stressful. Try to put yourself in situations where change is taking place, such as on a new work project or in a constantly innovating organization. Remind yourself that change is an opportunity for you or your organization to become even better. Yes... it's going to be stressful, but you will grow, and the further you challenge yourself, the more opportunity you allow yourself to grow into. Innovation sits at the nexus of change.

You can go one step further and be an agent of change once you feel at ease. You can practice and demonstrate your inventiveness and adaptability by looking for clever ways to shake things up, think outside the box, or facilitate necessary change, regardless of whether you are in charge.

4. **Integrity and Responsibility**: *A Willingness to Accept Responsibility*

As a leader, you are responsible not only for your own work but also for the work, attitude, and results of others. This is no easy task; you have to show your group where to go and what to do while supporting them, answering questions, tracking progress, and providing inspiration. Why? Because their failure is also your failure—their success is your success.

To develop this skill, start collaborating with at least one other person on a project, client campaign, or staff meeting. Offer support, answer questions, and ask how you can assist them. And if things don't go as planned, instead of trying to cover it up... you face your mistakes head on, and accept responsibility. Acknowledge what happened, apologize if the situation requires it, and do everything possible to correct course. Offer solutions to the problem and consider what you can learn from it in the future. By taking accountability, you demonstrate your character by showing up, acknowledging your error, and offering solutions. Being a leader often means taking responsibility for the bad and redirecting recognition to the team for the successes.

5. **Continual Learner**: *A Desire to Learn and Grow*

Even if you don't want to be a leader, a constant desire to learn and improve is an essential personal and professional trait. The best leaders always strive toward continual improvement because they are curious, ambitious, and invested in further growth for future opportunity.

Seek opportunities to learn more about how to be a leader in your daily life. Are you willing to take charge of an upcoming client campaign or team-building activity? Is there a leader you admire whom you could meet for coffee? Are there any leadership-related books or podcasts you can listen to in your spare time? Find ways to maximize opportunities for future potential.

There are numerous opportunities for learning, but you need the willingness and initiative to take advantage of them. Often, this is one of the most distinctive attributes that sets leaders apart from others.

Learning is a lifetime goal, and just like with all personal and professional growth, there will always be new ways to improve your talents, strengthen your skills, and find new opportunities to demonstrate leadership.

Putting it All Together

Leadership abilities are not typically inherited. A person who eventually becomes a great leader goes through a lot of learning (accompanied by a lot of experiential learning, often learning things "the hard way"). They research other leaders, attempt to learn and grow from their experience and identify other leaders to serve as role models. Naturally, great leaders can fail and should expect to because this is where growth occurs. However, the feedback they receive from various individuals can help them improve their skills after failure. This assists them with the ability to adapt into incredible leaders since they can change and readjust their behavior for the better.

Leaders often emerge from challenging circumstances, akin to coal undergoing intense pressure to transform into a diamond. They actively engage in reading, learning, and honing their skills through practice while seeking guidance to continuously enhance their abilities.

Regardless of whether a leader is created or born, development is the constant factor that determines success. While it is true that some leaders are born with personality traits that make leadership *easier*, effective leadership requires ongoing growth and development. You can always aim to be a better leader, no matter how far along you are in your professional career or how much success you've had.

Additional Thoughts

Are leaders created or born? The ability to exert influence over others in support of a leader's objectives, aims, or goals is a sign of leadership. A leader ought to recognize ways in which things can be improved and motivate others to work toward that improved vision; energize and positively influence those around them; work toward realizing their vision while prioritizing people; and should be able to empathize with others and connect with them for success. There has been a fascinating debate about whether leaders are made or born.

Chapter 11

The Science Behind a Successful, Efficient, and Productive Team

It is your responsibility as a team leader to ensure that your employees are achieving the company's goals and objectives. You should establish a system and an environment that enables them to work effectively, efficiently, and to the best of their abilities.

Navigating change requires significant effort. During times of change, teams often face challenges in taking the initial steps toward embracing new ways of working. They may feel uncertain, overwhelmed, or resistant to change. As a leader, your support plays a crucial role in helping them navigate this transition. By providing guidance, resources, and encouragement, you can empower your employees to take the necessary actions to initiate change. Empower your team members to cultivate productive habits that foster focus and enable comprehensive decision-making within the constraints of time and deadlines.

However, encouraging your team to become more effective and efficient alone does not suffice. You must also take additional measures to position them for success. Most employees are not purposefully wasteful or neglectful with their time. Often, they simply require a little more assistance or alignment with an understanding of expectations in order to execute their work with excellence. This is where core concepts around motivation, incentive, and purpose play a pivotal role.

Explain to the team that you want them to work more effectively and give them resources and opportunities to do so. Tell them how much work they should finish in a typical shift and give advice on how to do that work well. Explain to them how they can improve the quality of their work if there is a problem with their effectiveness. This is all consistent with setting clear expectations and building team alignment.

Training shouldn't be considered a one-time opportunity limited to the onboarding phase. I find it works best to intentionally schedule training sessions to talk about how to work more effectively and efficiently where the opportunity exists. This is a great way to remind employees of important information they may have overlooked, and you can use this time to introduce new plans they can use to make their work easier.

Set up weekly, biweekly, or monthly meetings to monitor your team's progress once you have implemented a system for increased productivity. This serves two purposes. First, so you can engage with each person and gauge their current activities, but more importantly it offers a way to ensure you are still engaged with each employee at a personal level. Yes, this is super challenging sometimes, but it adds value to each person at a personal level – and it is an incredibly valuable part of building and nurturing a team.

Each person needs to know they are valued and their skillset adds a unique and valuable advantage to the team and company for the work they are performing. Showing a team member gratitude and appreciation has to be genuine for the connection to resonate. This is the one area that can highlight strengths, expose weaknesses, or depreciate a leader's ability to influence as a true leader over the long term. Learning how to value people is a key leadership attribute. So learn to listen, be empathetic, learn to relate, and learn how to value others.

Evaluating Employees

Some of the most important aspects to evaluate and target during your conversations with employees are:

- The quality of each team member's work, in order to determine how it adds value to your business.

- Consistency with their quality and delivery and identifying areas to adjust where necessary in order to align with goals.

- The time it takes to finish their work on an average day, month, or quarter. This helps provide better future estimates to align with ongoing work.

Showing and Not Just Telling

Setting an intentional example is essential when leading a productive and efficient team. If you want them to increase their productivity, then you should assist them in doing so. By offering your help, you are establishing a culture that encourages teams to develop their skills and grow professionally.

Leaders who want to cultivate a high-performance team must recognize that it goes beyond merely assembling a group of talented individuals. It requires a deliberate and strategic approach to shape team culture and provide unwavering support to each team member. By fostering an environment that encourages collaboration, innovation, and continuous growth, leaders create fertile ground for greatness to flourish.

A great leader understands the interplay between individual strengths, fostering open communication, and cultivating a shared sense of purpose between the team toward a common goal. Through these deliberate actions, leaders ignite the spark that propels a team from good to exceptional. It requires a deep-rooted transformation in the very fabric of the company's culture. Nurturing an environment that fosters collaboration, trust, and open communication becomes foundational upon which exceptional teams are built. By crafting an ecosystem that ignites passion, unleashes creativity, and nurtures individual growth, leaders can harness the full potential of their teams and achieve remarkable feats that defy expectations. These teams navigate challenges with ease, turning them into opportunities for growth.

Great Teams are Connected Teams

A majority of high-performance teams have similar characteristics, whether we're talking about elite special operations units, successful professional sports teams, or highly effective business organizations. They have resilient mindsets, are better able to adapt to change, and have higher levels of internal trust and accountability. These teams are longer-lasting, have a higher level of engagement, and are, therefore, more productive. High-performance businesses have higher levels of employee and customer satisfaction and retention, grow more speedily (and intelligently), and are more profitable

(Gleeson 2019). They also operate under a clear mission narrative.

Customer experience, employee satisfaction, and operational performance are just a few areas where research shows that teams almost always make better decisions than individuals.

Connected teams are 21% more profitable than unconnected teams. Absenteeism is reduced by 41%, employee turnover is reduced by 59%, and employee wellness is improved by 66% in teams ranked in the top 20% for connectedness. Even if they weren't satisfied with their jobs, 37% of employees cited "working with a great team" as their primary reason for staying with an organization.

To build a high-performance team, there are at minimum three psychological needs that must be met:

Autonomy: People are empowered when they feel supported and able to choose their own course of action. Autonomy and independence are two distinct concepts in how individuals approach their work. Autonomy allows for voluntary action and choice, whether working alone or with others while maintaining a sense of intrinsic motivation. Independence, on the other hand, implies a preference for working alone without relying on others. Recognizing and fostering autonomy can empower individuals to make choices aligned with their strengths and motivations while promoting collaboration when needed.

Competence: The idea that people want to control how things turn out and that this control lets them master a task or a particular area. People's intrinsic motivation to complete the task increases when they receive unexpectedly positive feedback.

Relatedness: Humans are social creatures who need to interact with other people. Through social connections and a strong concern for others, this sense of relatedness is shown. According to self-determination theory, intrinsic motivation is linked to individuals' relatedness.

Cultivating High-Performance Teams

Teams that embody the following characteristics are poised for remarkable success:

Organized and Goal Focused: To achieve results, the team works under specific deadlines, which requires setting goals. When setting goals, a SMART goal can be used as an excellent guide. Specific, Measurable, Achievable, Realistic, and Timely. A SMART goal incorporates all of these elements to help you concentrate on the task at hand and boosts your chances of success.

Culture of Accountability: In addition to emphasizing the significance of accountability, the organization has established frameworks that link experiences, beliefs, and actions to desired business outcomes.

Seamless Communication: Everybody puts forth unprecedented attempts to guarantee high levels of clear and open communication. When the right tools are used, deliberately creating formal and casual systems for sharing data across the organization becomes easier.

Comfort Zone Expansion (*and continual passion towards continued growth*): The team's work goes beyond their comfort zone. They take calculated risks and constantly consider: "What if?" Adversity is welcomed and embraced by the team.

Ecosystems, Not Hierarchies: Leadership and decision-making are more decentralized in high-performance teams. While the arranging system normally stays concentrated and zeroed in on higher perspective procedures, the execution of assignments and obligations is decentralized. The hierarchy moves leadership down the chain of command.

Proper Planning: For planning and carrying out tasks, the team has appropriate mechanisms and standard operating procedures. They include all appropriate team members in the planning process and solicit their feedback and participation. Everyone's voice is heard.

Introspection/Retrospective: To determine how processes can be enhanced and what lessons can be shared with other members, the team stops at appropriate times to examine the quality of its most recent work. A center of excellence keeps a record of the results of the after-action review process, which is carried out regularly.

High Participation: To ensure everyone is involved, members work hard. Participation is driven by involvement. Very few team members are disengaged.

Self-Managed: Team leadership shifts according to the required level of expertise. As flaws or gaps are discovered, team members step in. This capability is reinforced by a good leader and enables the team to jump in.

Trust is Measured: The group is aware that trust directly affects profitability, engagement, and productivity. Trustworthiness, genuineness, and straightforwardness (in the proper time and place) are essential to creating normal conduct standards.

Guiding Principles: The team's behavior and communication are governed by a specific and clearly defined set of guiding principles. A common language is used as part of the organization's "way." For talent acquisition, promotion efforts, and reward mechanisms, guiding principles are always taken into consideration.

Celebrates Success: High-performance teams celebrate small victories on the way to achieving their goals. Team members collaborate to strengthen one another. They care deeply about everyone else's circumstances and self-improvement. Acknowledging progress is key in building a team's morale and proves highly important in the long-term strategy for trust building, relationship building, and communication.

Leaders have a profound impact on the success of both employees and the organization. Employees look to their leaders for direction, coaching, support, and feedback, and leaders who fall short in any of these areas risk both their employees' satisfaction and their own reputation.

Teams tend to be more engaged when they are enthusiastic about their work. The passion they exhibit comes naturally because they love what they are pursuing. They are committed to their employer, frequently willing to put in extra effort and contribute to enhancing their employer's good name through positive word-of-mouth communication (Birt 2023). Leaders can directly affect employee engagement by showing concern for their employees at a personal level. The benefit becomes increasingly evident over time and helps build a much more stable trust level between the team. In the pursuit of this, it is beneficial to enable employees to openly communicate and voice their ideas, and commend employees for a job well done.

There are numerous ways in which leaders have a direct and indirect impact on their employee's productivity. For instance, a leader with poor planning abilities will make it difficult for employees to meet deadlines, which will eventually lead to a decline in productivity because employees will become less motivated the more unrealistic the deadline is. In a similar vein, a leader who makes use of their authority to delegate responsibilities runs the risk of putting too much on staff, resulting in lower levels of output. Note: often the deficits of poor leadership take a long time to surface—the unraveled mess it can leave can be compounded over time.

Putting it All Together

It would be a mistake to attribute all improvements in a team solely to team leader performance. Team improvements are more likely to result from a partnership between the team and the leader. However, a leader is a catalyst for this.

Trust, respect, and loyalty are typically developed in groups by team leaders who score highly on mutual respect and camaraderie. They make it possible and encourage having difficult discussions and debates about business issues. They have integrity, which drives them to do as they say and say what they mean. Conflict is made productive by these leaders, which has a positive effect on team behavior and collaboration. They consider other people's points of view and carefully weigh what they say.

Stability and consistency are the qualities I admire most in leaders because wise and knowledgeable leaders produce these qualities. Until it is absent, stability is not something we often consider a leadership quality. Consider the worst possible leader and reflect on what attributes you tend to think they convey. Poor leaders tend to exhibit erratic behavior and inconsistent actions, which tend to cause unnecessary tension, anxiety, and conflict – resulting in a lack of trust due to the inability to convey stability and consistency. Growth is harmed, productivity is stifled, trust is eroded, and it is extremely difficult to concentrate on the task at hand when there is a lack of stability. Instability also indicates larger issues to come.

On the other hand, when leaders demonstrate stability and consistency, it reinforces a calming influence on those within their sphere of impact and provides valuable support and a sense of security. These leaders often display attributes such as being trustworthy, admirable, and dependable. The certainty and consistency that teams and organizations desperately require but frequently lack are brought about by leaders who instill stability. By distributing accurate information, cultivating optimism, and having a clear vision, leaders focus their concentration on the team's stability.

Digging deeper: Case study research

In the heart of England, a remarkable tale unfolded on the football pitch that captured the world's attention. It was the story of Leicester City Football Club, a team that defied the odds and achieved the impossible. At the center of this remarkable journey was the transformative power of leadership.

Under the guidance of Claudio Ranieri, the team's manager, Leicester City experienced a true metamorphosis. Ranieri instilled a sense of belief within the players, forging an unbreakable bond that would prove instrumental in their success. He cultivated a culture of teamwork, unity, and resilience, where every player felt valued and embraced their role. Ranieri's leadership brought about a tactical revolution. He recognized the team's strengths and adapted their playing style to maximize their potential. With a careful balance of strategy and flexibility, he harnessed the collective talent of the squad and unleashed it on the pitch. Players who were previously overlooked or undervalued discovered newfound confidence, as they realized the power of teamwork and the impact it could have.

As the season progressed, Leicester City's rise from underdogs to title contenders captivated the world. Their triumph was not just a result of skill but a testament to the transformative impact of leadership. In the face of adversity, they persevered. Every player fought for one another, fueled by a shared vision and the unwavering belief instilled by their leader.

The climax came when Leicester City lifted the Premier League trophy, etching their name in football history. It was a moment that symbolized the triumph of teamwork, dedication, and exceptional leadership. Their story stands as a testament to the profound importance of leadership in teams. It reminds us that with the right guidance, belief, and unity, even the most unlikely dreams can become a reality.

Leicester City's journey showcases that leadership is the catalyst that transforms a group of individuals into a cohesive and high-performing team. It highlights the significance of fostering a positive team culture, adapting strategies to leverage strengths, instilling belief, and nurturing resilience. The tale of Leicester City Football Club serves as a timeless reminder that great leadership is the key that unlocks the full potential of teams, propelling them to achieve extraordinary results.

ADDITIONAL THOUGHTS

The amount of high-impact works your team can accomplish by removing workplace friction and distractions is called team efficiency. Team efficiency is not about being productive for the sake of being productive, it is about how to build an efficient workplace and promote healthy teamwork in the workplace to boost team performance as a whole.

Leaders bring stability and consistency to the team, creating a sense of security and support. Their presence and guidance have a direct impact on team members, shaping their behaviors, attitudes, and performance. A leader's influence sets the tone for the team, inspiring and motivating them to achieve their goals. By leveraging their influence effectively, leaders can foster a positive and productive team environment, leading to enhanced collaboration, growth, and success.

Trust enables effective communication and collaboration. Team members are more likely to share their ideas, concerns, and feedback when they trust that their leader will listen and consider their perspectives. This fosters a culture of open dialogue, creativity, and innovation.

Chapter 12

The Measure of Success

Your career objectives will largely determine how you evaluate your workplace success. While supervisors or employers may use regular performance reviews or metrics to assess employee success, defining what success means to you and how you will achieve it is the first step in tracking your progress.

To embark on a new endeavor successfully, you must have a comprehensive grasp of the project's scope and its alignment with your department's and company's objectives. By collectively identifying the team's objectives and aspirations, you can define the performance criteria that will drive success and progress toward shared goals.

A measure of *success* is a standard by which an individual or organization determines whether they have attained their *objectives*. Successful people (in the sense of business "success") use multiple benchmarks to evaluate their personal and professional accomplishments because there is no standard measure of success.

Even though some achievement metrics are more prevalent than others, they are all at least somewhat subjective or relative. For instance, even the highest-earning businesses might have a stifling organizational culture, overworked executives, and a high rate of employee turnover. Due to the high earning potential, some people might consider such a business a *success,* while others might argue that it does not hit their objective goals or definition of success due to its inability to create a positive work environment. There are limitless combinations of what success looks like, and it is highly dependent on your intended goals. This makes the definition of "success" that much more of a relative interpretation.

Ultimately, how you define your primary organizational goals determines how you measure success. While you should set goals that align with the company's overall priorities, your personal and professional measures of success should make sense to you and your team. In addition, success can be measured by a variety of metrics. For instance, making record profits and ensuring that your workers enjoy coming to work may not be mutually exclusive objectives.

There are at least two more general methods for evaluating success in terms of *quality* and *quantity*. By looking at overarching trends within your organization that may be difficult to quantify, you can qualitatively measure success. Quantitative success, on the other hand, is measured by looking at specific metrics, data points, and similar criteria to see how well you're meeting your goals.

As a leader, your victories are those of your team. A good leader is most content when their teams or employees thrive, and they know how to give them the tools, resources, and support needed to succeed.

Many organizational leaders struggle to answer this crucial question about themselves in an organizational culture obsessed with management by metrics. It can be tempting to judge leaders solely by how well their businesses perform. However, even the most successful founders are aware of the extent to which opportunistic chance and timing can muddle this strategy. To extend the concept, there is no simple way to gauge a person's leadership potential by measuring bottom-line company performance. So, is there a better approach?

You can be an effective leader if you can think and communicate clearly, make sound decisions about other people, and keep your own integrity and commitment. This method of establishing trust is both a *science* and an *art*, which is why competence and character are required. When leaders clearly plan for the future and steer their organizations in the right direction in terms of product, sales, and people, trust can be built. Do the predictions you create about the future, such as which products you should develop, which investments you should make, and how the technological or competitive landscape will change, turn out to be accurate? And do the people you've chosen to run your business prove to be the right people? These questions and answers become known over time, and if you answer many of them correctly, you will gain trust as a leader. This is the foundational science behind establishing trust. It is based on the principles of clear thinking, effective communication, and sound judgment when it comes to understanding and interacting with others.

Building trust can be quite a difficult skill to master. It is inextricably linked to a leader's capacity for honest communication. Empathy and objectively sound judgment build trust when combined with conveying the right details at the correct time. It grows when you put your personal success, interests, reputation, or position aside and stand for goals bigger than you. It also grows when you are open and vulnerable with others. This uniqueness you offer is essentially what has helped shape the skills you have, and you can use that to your advantage as you continue to refine your leadership skills.

Most great leaders know how to build trust. They know that when they hire and promote people to leadership positions, they need to think clearly about product and strategy, communicate clearly, and make sound decisions. They know they need to put in a lot of effort and follow through fully. However, the truly great leaders we observe also know how to *cultivate* trust. Leaders must make many difficult decisions, such as firing employees, taking responsibility for shortcomings, disappointing people by saying no, etc. These difficulties are viewed by great leaders as *opportunities* to increase trust. Shaping perceptions of otherwise negative situations and shifting them into a positive opportunistic view can prove incredibly beneficial. Truly extraordinary leaders ask themselves which strategy and method of communication will boost the team's confidence and enable them to succeed personally and professionally. The key here is the ability to maximize trust when faced with difficult challenges.

Perhaps this is the lesson that great leaders impart to others: in challenging and trying times, when faced with a choice between two options, consider which one will enhance trust in you as a leader. Make it your constant endeavor to choose that path.

During my professional career I spent and inordinate amount of time and effort striving toward "success", (*or more appropriately, what I thought success was at the time*), and I imagine I am not alone in this sentiment. But one sentiment that I have come to understand clearer is the disparity between the meaning and the definition of "success", as defined by everyone else *for me*. I have reached the conclusion the idea of success does not reside in meeting an ever-shifting ideation as defined by the influences around me for their definition of success, which are ones based on wealth and social status, and rather shift my focus to what is best for my current team and our goals. In order to do so I utilize the following principals:

QUANTIFYING PEOPLE IS A PARADOX UNRIVALED

The concepts behind a quantified ranking is directly connected to the common definition of success, but a confined one. We use a variety of metrics to quantify and put numbers on people in the quantified outlook, such as salary, grades, social-media likes, followers, home size, and so on. Someone is said to be more successful if they score higher on those metrics.

According to research, the human brain immediately loses its natural desire to explore, experiment, and learn when ranking metrics like these are introduced. In one study, a Salk Institute team led by Howard Hughes Medical Institute researcher Dr. Kay Tye examined the activity in the brains of mice as they competed to drink a sweet liquid. Mice were kept together by the team until a social order was established. The researchers then taught each mouse on its own that when a sound was played, the liquid would appear in the cage. The researchers then monitored the mice's brain activity as they competed for two at a time to drink the liquid. In general, dominant mice consumed more liquid than subordinate mice.

During the competition, the researchers discovered that the opposing mouse's social rank influenced the neurons' activity in the medial prefrontal cortex (mPFC). A mouse's social ranking could be predicted with 90% accuracy based on brain activity in the mPFC. These brain patterns were also able to predict which mouse would win the competition before it even started. Although the dominant mice frequently emerged victorious, this was not always the case. This suggests that motivation and self-assurance were other factors that contributed. (Reynolds 2022)

Granted this was a study observing mice, not humans, but it helps to provide context. We start chasing numbers and turn life into a competition rather than following the explorative mindset that occurs naturally. In other words, we easily dismiss our natural intuitive senses and instead spend time competing for equally artificial things in a manufactured system.

Therefore, success, as defined by that definition, is *created* and does not exist outside of a bias understanding of the term.

LIFE AS A COMPETITION = A LIFE DRIVEN BY FEAR

You don't have to look far to find someone that views life as a competition. Its an alluring trap to get caught up into. We want to be wealthier, stronger, smarter, healthier, more well-known, and more glamorous than everyone else. That innate desire is rooted and primarily motivated by fear, and when pursued it is easy to loose sight of the truly important factors.

Being consumed by losing can put a lot of pressure on the person as they only expect winning as their outcome. The majority of us simply do not want to lose, according to the competition-based definition of life success. It's as if each of us has a mental scoreboard where we rank and compare ourselves, our friends, friends of friends, celebrities, and even imagined versions of ourselves (who we wish we were). Because we are utterly terrified that our names will be at the bottom of that scoreboard, we compete for money, relevancy, and social status.

All of the following are common scenarios we hear internally when fear kicks in:

- *I might lose my job if I perform below my peers.*
- *I might not be able to maintain my lifestyle if I lose my job.*
- *I might have to relocate somewhere cheaper if I can't afford my lifestyle.*
- *They might not respect me if X happens, and I might end up all by myself.*

The cycle continues until you either rationalize or defeat that fear. We compete out of fear of all those theoretical "maybes" and many more. In the end, with this mentality, all that matters to us is the never-ending, fear-based competition in which everyone competes and is under unsustainable pressure. We are too scared to resist and choose a better option, allowing the fear to overtake objective reasoning.

THE FALLACY OF: 'MY SUCCESS SHOULD BE MY OWN'

A true leader reflects the success of the team back to the team. Building your team up and putting yourself aside is of primary importance, but in the self-seeking interest of success it sometimes gets lost. In reality, in a team structure, a leader's success is entirely dependent on other people's achievements and/or accomplishments. The altruistic view we find too often in business deters our vantage, and skews our ability to treat others in a loving and respectable way. This school of thought, in terms of 'my success should be my own' is one of the surest ways to demise in a team over the long term.

People are drawn to new ideas, innovative products, services, songs, or stories because they aid in their own personal life exploration, in return distracting you from your God given purpose, which is where success truly resides. Living life in the purpose for which you were created for is where we truly discover the key to success. Don't fall into the trap of letting others define your idea of success. It's not in how you compare to other people that should provide your sense of success, and because of this, success is never a competition.

You will face leadership challenges on a daily basis, from a multitude of angles, and even from within. True leadership—one that is founded on integrity, authenticity, and meaningful relationships—requires courageousness. It takes a great deal of hard work to be a leader who can motivate others, serve them, and guide them toward a greater goal and vision. The path to leadership is not without its challenges. Sometimes they appear to be obstacles. Sometimes the bridge completely fails. However, every obstacle can be viewed as an opportunity. It's a chance to learn more about yourself, continue to refine/build your skills, and build your emotional intelligence, which are all pivotally important for great leadership.

These obstacles, when turned into opportunities, can be some of the most beneficial intersections for impact. The skill to make a difference in the lives of others is at the heart of leadership. When you start with that, you can create an atmosphere where people are interested, motivated, and genuinely care – in which they can really collaborate, solve problems together, and care about each other.

"*Leadership is a choice. It is not a rank.*" - Simon Sinek

Throughout the book, we have explored the leadership challenges from many vantage points. We have discovered that great leadership may begin with the leader, but it truly flows from the team. Leadership is a choice to prioritize the needs of others in order to construct a strong and cohesive team. As we conclude this journey, let this book serve as a catalyst for your growth as a remarkable leader, armed with the knowledge and inspiration to make a lasting impact. As you reflect on the insights and strategies shared, step into becoming the leader your team truly needs, making a lasting impact on their success and growth. Embrace the challenges and let your leadership abilities transform not only your own life but also the lives of those around you. By embracing the principles and practices we've explored, you will be well-equipped to create positive change and overcome any challenge that comes our way through the collective potential of the team. The impact we make goes beyond ourselves - it resonates within every team member, propelling us toward extraordinary outcomes. You can overcome any obstacle with impactful leadership.

Additional Thoughts

Without defining success, measuring it can be challenging, if not impossible. While definitions of success in business may vary from person to person, achieving your teams desired goals can provide valuable insight to allow you to find success in your business and leadership goals in a way that resonates with your values and aspirations. You must create some kind of measurement for success so you can see how you are doing in both your personal and professional ventures, even if your methods are different from those of others.

Closing Statements

One of the best pieces of advice I can offer is that a great team doesn't happen overnight; you can't just walk into a situation and fix everything simply by making a few tweaks and expect that within a few days, everything will get better. It requires a lot of work through small changes, patience, and learning from each other over a long period of time. Leaders are in it for the long-haul. It takes strategic and well-coordinated effort, having the discipline to make adjustments when necessary while understanding the intended goals, and putting in the hard work to get the team to the envisioned destination.

Only by pride cometh contention: but with the well advised is wisdom. - Proverbs 13:10

References

(Zippia), Kristin Kizer. 2023. *36 Powerful Leadership Statistics [2023]: Things All Aspiring Leaders Should Know.* Feburary. https://www.zippia.com/advice/leadership-statistics/#:~:text=78%25%20of%20business%20leaders%20actively,cultivated%20into%20high%2Dquality%20leadership.

Akorede, Shakir. 2018. *Three Things To Learn From Google's Workplace Culture.* https://www.entrepreneur.com/en-ae/growth-strategies/three-things-to-learn-from-googles-workplace-culture/317582.

Apollo Technical. 2022. *Leadership Development Statistics.* https://www.apollotechnical.com/leadership-statistics/#:~:text=their%20stress%20levels.-,Leadership%20Development%20Statistics,develop%20leaders%20at%20all%20levels.

Birt, Jamie. 2023. *10 Qualities of a Good Employee (With Examples).* Mar 16. https://www.indeed.com/career-advice/career-development/good-employee-qualities.

Boundless. 2016. *Choosing Team Size and Team Members.* May 26. https://www.boundless.com/management/textbooks/boundless-management-textbook/groups-teams-and-teamwork-6/building-successful-teams-53/choosing-team-size-and-team-members-268-3956/ Source: Boundless. "Choosing Team Size and Team Members." Boundless Manage.

Brandenburger, Adam M., and Barry J. Nalebuff. 1996. *Co-opetition.* New York: Doubleday.

Collins, Jim. n.d. *First who, Then what...* Accessed 2023. https://www.jimcollins.com/concepts/first-who-then-what.html.

—. n.d. *Good to Great.* London, England: Random House Business Books.

Dilenschneider, Robert L. 1992. *A Briefing for Leaders: Communication As the Ultimate Exercise of Power.*

Encyclopedia for Business. n.d. *Game Theory.* https://www.referenceforbusiness.com/encyclopedia/For-Gol/Game-Theory.html.

Gillett, Rachel. 2016. *A high percentage of Googlers say they're satisfied in their job.* https://www.businessinsider.com/google-is-the-best-company-to-work-for-in-america-2016-4#a-high-percentage-of-googlers-say-theyresatisfied-in-their-job-1.

Gitlow, Abraham L. 2004. *Being the Boss: The Importance of Leadership and Power.*

Gleeson, Brent. 2019. *15 Characteristics Of High-Performance Teams.* Mar 14. https://www.forbes.com/sites/brentgleeson/2019/03/14/15-

characteristics-of-high-performance-teams/?sh=410b4f3e6ae0.

Goleman, Daniel. 2005. *Emotional Intelligence: Why It Can Matter More Than IQ.*

Horn, Art. 1997. *Gifts of Leadership : Team-Building Through Focus and Empathy.*

Kristin Ryba - Quantum Workplace. 2021. *How to Align Individual, Team, and Organizational Goals for Success.* https://www.quantumworkplace.com/future-of-work/how-to-align-organizational-goals.

Landry, Lauren. 2019. *Why emotional intelligence is important in leadership.* Apr 3. https://online.hbs.edu/blog/post/emotional-intelligence-in-leadership.

Li, Lori. 2022. *17 Surprising Statistics about Employee Retention.* April 8. https://www.tinypulse.com/blog/17-surprising-statistics-about-employee-retention.

Muse, Tyler. 2019. *Are leaders born or made?* Oct 22. https://www.hrdconnect.com/are-leaders-born-or-made/.

O. C. Tanner. n.d. *How does leadership influence organizational culture?* https://www.octanner.com/insights/articles/2019/10/23/how_does_leadership_.html#:~:text=What%20Aspects%20of%20Company%20Culture,inspiration%20to%20those%20they%20lead.

Olsen, Terra Clarke. n.d. *Consequences of Hiring the Wrong Employee and Tips for Making a Better Hire.* https://www.akkencloud.com/consequences-hiring-wrong-employee/.

Osborn, Alex F. 1953. *Applied Imagination: Principles and Procedures of Creative Thinking.*

Reynolds, Sharon. 2022. *Understanding how the brain tracks social status and competition.* April 12. https://www.nih.gov/news-events/nih-research-matters/understanding-how-brain-tracks-social-status-competition.

Ries, Eric. 2011. *The Lean Startup: How Today's Entrepreneurs Use Continuous Innovation to Create Radically Successful Businesses.* New York: Crown Business.

Tank, Aytekin. 2023. *Productivity Is More about Mind-Management than Time-Management.* Jan 27. https://www.jotform.com/blog/productivity-is-more-about-mind-management-than-time-management/.

VisioneerIT. n.d. *Growth vs Scaling: What does your business demand?* https://www.visioneerit.com/blog/growth-vs-scaling-business-demand.

www.ingramcontent.com/pod-product-compliance
Lightning Source LLC
Chambersburg PA
CBHW052346220526
45465CB00003BA/982